Recovery From Narcissistic Abuse

A Practical Work Book by Survivors

Dr Shé D'Montford et al.

Recovery From Narcissistic Abuse - A Practical Work Book by Survivors © 2022

All rights reserved. No part of this book may be reproduced in any form or by any electronic or mechanical means, including information storage and retrieval systems, without permission in writing from the author.

This book was professionally written, edited, and formatted. It is not a pre-published work and remains the copyrighted property of the author.

The information provided in this book is designed to provide helpful information on the subjects discussed. The author's books are only meant to provide the reader with the basic knowledge of specific topics without any guarantees concerning results. This book is for educational and entertainment purposes only. While most care has been taken in compiling the information contained in this book, no responsibility can be accepted by the author for any errors or omissions that may be made. Neither can any liability be accepted by the publisher for any damages, losses, or costs resulting from using the information contained within these pages.

All trademarks and registered trademarks appearing in this book are the property of their respective owners and are used only to describe the products being provided directly. Every effort has been made to capitalise, punctuate, identify, and attribute trademarks and register where appropriate according to industry standards.

Written By Dr. Shé D'Montford

Research Credit Dr Mariam Farooq

A huge thank you to the many who have had the courage to share their stories with me over the years. Especially Joei B, for sharing her stories of the narcissist we shared.
Recovery and thrival (not just survival) happen when you reach out.

Table Of Contents

Foreword — 8
- Step One: Understanding — 9
- Why Empaths Are So Vulnerable — 11
- My Story In Brief: From Survival to "Thrival" — 12
- Why This Workbook Exists — 16
- Justice, Healing, and True "Revenge" — 18
- Success is the best revenge. — 19
- From Survival to "Thrival" — 20

Preface — 22
- This Is a 'Victims of Narcissists' Recovery Work Book — 23

What Is Narcissism? — 26
- A Spectrum Of Narcissism — 27
- Narcissistic Personality Disorder — 28

Narcissism in the Modern Age — 34
- The Different Types Of Narcissists — 35

Your Relationship — 38

with a Narcissist — 38
- Identifying The Narcissistic Relationship — 40
  - The Fairy-Tale Start — 41
  - Conversation Hogging — 41
  - The Cravings for Compliments — 42
  - A Lack of Empathy — 42
  - Unreasonable Expectations — 43
  - A Need for Control — 43
  - Lack of Meaningful Long-Term Friendships or Relationships — 44
  - Gaslighting — 44
  - Aggressiveness at Hearing a No — 45

- Survival Technique 1 — 45
- Identifying Your Abuser as a Potential Narcissist — 45
- One-Sided Listening — 46
- One-Sided Vision — 47
- NRA - No Rules Apply — 48
- Super-Sensitivity to Criticisms — 49
- Blaming Others — 50
- Lack of Appreciation — 51

| Quick to Anger and Anger is Blamed on Your Actions . . . | 52 |

Self-Blame and Self-Doubt — 54

- Survival Technique 2 — 58
- Gaslighting Gauge — 58
- Consciously Countering Self-Doubt — 59

Who Was Narcissus? — 62
- Immaturity and Rehabilitation — 66

Who Was Echo? — 72
- Echo and Narcissus — 74

- Survival Technique 3 — 83
- Echo Method — 83

Why Echo Fell For a Narcissist — 88
- Narcissists don't fall in love. — 88
- Narcissists need helpful people around them. — 89
- Narcissists seek out altruistic people. — 90
- Narcissists look for victims who have already been victims. — 91

The Narcissistic Parent — 94
- Engulfing Narcissists — 94
- Using Narcissists — 95
- Ignoring Narcissists — 96

- Survival Technique 4 — 101
- Identifying The Narcissistic Parent — 101
- Did you have a narcissistic mother and/or father? — 101

Healing Your Inner Child — 108
- Grey Rock — 110
- Silence — 111

- Survival Technique 5 — 112
- Assessing Responsibility to an Abusive Parent — 112
- Earning Forgiveness — 115

- Survival Technique 6 — 118
- A Journey to Your Inner Child — 118

- Survival Technique 7 — 123

Narcissism Self-Check — 123
How well a person listens to others is a primary indicator of narcissism. — 126
Bilateral Listening — 126
Generosity — 127

Narcissistic Religions and Cults — 132
The Author's Story — 134
1) The Cult's Charismatic Founder or Chieftains are Narcissists — 148
2) Cults Are Very Loving at First — 150
3) Cults Practice Brainwashing — 150
4) Cults Isolate the Individual — 153
5) Cults and Narcissists Do Not Respect Personal Boundaries — 154
6) Cults Seek to Control Situations and People — 155
7) Cults Seek to Make You Fully Dependant Upon Them — 157
8) Cults Punish Non-Compliance — 159
Thought-Terminating Cult Clichés — 160

Infamous Cults From The Past and Present — 162
The Manson Family — 162
The Peoples Temple — 163
The Aum Shinrikyo — 163
The Branch Davidians — 164
Klu Klux Klan — 166
The Nazi Party — 167
ISIS / ISIL — 168

Cult Check List — 170
Narcissist Check List — 172
Escaping the Cult — 173
1) No Contact — 174
2) Build Your Self-Trust and Self-Esteem — 175
3) Reach Out For Support and Help — 175

Stepping Out of — 178

Victim Consciousness — 178
Survival Technique 8 — 181
Recognising Your Victim Status — 181
Honesty With the Self Through Myth — 182
Identifying Your Victim Status — 187

Recovery Check List — 192
Get away from your abuser(s) — 192
Get Help — 193

Survival Technique 9	**194**
Honest Self Assessment of 'Assets' and 'Needs' Here and Now	**194**
Personal and Immediate Resource Directory	**198**
List Support Contacts	198
Supportive friends or family members	198
Local Police Domestic Violence Unit	199
A professional counsellor or volunteer professional	200
Work: Colleagues & Bosses	201
Child Care	203
Food - Clothing - Shelter	203
Legal Representative or Legal Aid	205
Implement Self-Care	**206**
Breathe	206
Be Creative	207
Change You Self-View	208
Something fun for you to do on your own or with a friend	209
A spoil or pamper thing for you to do when you are feeling stressed or deserve a reward. 210	
Detox from Abuse	**210**
Detox From Toxic People	210
Write your feelings in a journal	212
Exercise	213
Diet	214
Meditation	215
Mindfulness	215
Limit the use of technology	217
Sleep	218
Thrive	**219**
Survival Technique 10	**222**
Share Your Personal Stories	**222**
Shé's Story	224
Jo and Shé Support Each Other	244
Jo's Story	254
Bill's Story	266
Lillian's Story	277
Can a Narcissist	**296**
Change and Recover?	**296**
The Consequences of Staying With a Narcissist	**297**
Self-Worth	298
Emotional Abuse	298
Guilt	299
Isolation	299
Can Anything Be Done?	**300**
Open Communication	300
Boundaries	301

Keep Your Expectations Realistic	301
Focus on the Positive	302
Helping Them to Change	302
Quick Fixes	303
Training Your Partner to Calm Down	**304**
Training Your Partner to Listen	**307**

Last Resort   314
Keep Your Love to Yourself for a While   314
Do Not Lose Hope   316

After Word   318

Foreword

If you're holding this book, there's a good chance you feel like you've been struggling to keep your head above water. Life with a narcissist feels like being tossed around in a storm: exhausting, confusing, and often terrifying.

This book is a lifeline. Not a magic wand, not a quick fix —but a steady hand to help guide you from those troubled waters back to calmer, safer shores.

I'm not going to ask you to fix everything at once. That's too much for anyone, especially for someone who has already been coping with far too much, for far too long. Instead, we start small. We start simple. We start with three gentle but powerful steps.

Think of this book as your first *bite-size chunk* of recovery. You didn't get into this situation overnight, and you won't get out overnight either. But step by step, little by little, you *can* move from simply surviving… to truly thriving.

Step One: Understanding

Before anything else, you need to know this:

- You are **not** imagining things.
- You are **not** overreacting.
- You are **not** alone.

There are ordinary "bad" relationships, and then there are narcissistic relationships. Narcissistic relationships are in a category of their own.

In a narcissistic relationship, arguments and verbal abuse become the norm. They might not happen every day, but when they do, they are vicious and unprovoked. Simply having a different opinion, wanting to make a choice for yourself, or not complying with what your partner wants can trigger an explosion.

These arguments are not random. They are a tool. They are used to manipulate you, to blame you, and to teach you that your needs and views are dangerous or wrong.

Narcissists come in all genders. Narcissism is absolutely gender-neutral.

At the same time, we live in a culture that often encourages self-focus and "me first" thinking. We are told that if someone disagrees with us, they are invalidating us. But a healthy relationship is not one where two people always think the same. That would be boring.

Healthy relationships are built on **difference plus compromise**.

Two people with different opinions working together to find a third option that honours both of them. That's partnership. That's relating. It's not always easy, but it is respectful, safe, and mutual.

A narcissistic relationship is the opposite of that. There is no true compromise. There is only one opinion that is allowed to exist in the room, and if you challenge it, you pay the price. Personal attacks, gaslighting, threats, and sometimes physical violence become part of the emotional rollercoaster. That is *never* acceptable in any relationship.

Why Empaths Are So Vulnerable

The typical pattern is heartbreakingly familiar: an empath or deeply caring and sensitive person becomes the ideal target for a narcissist.

Empaths are naturally forgiving. They see the best in people. They explain away red flags as "stress" or "a bad day" or "my fault." At first, they believe they are just being kind and understanding.

The narcissist knows they can't show their worst behaviour straight away—no one would stay. So the cruelty comes in increments. A cutting remark here. A cruel joke there. A sudden rage outburst. A guilt trip. Then an apology. Then a little bit worse. And a little bit worse again.

Slowly, your boundaries are boiled away, just like a lobster in cold water that's heated so gradually it doesn't realise it's in danger until it's too late.

By the time many empaths realise that something is very wrong, they are in far too deep. Isolated. Confused. Ashamed. Exhausted.

If that's you, please know: this is not a sign of your weakness. It is a sign of your capacity to love, trust, and forgive—and those are beautiful qualities. This book will help you protect those qualities, instead of letting them be used against you.

My Story In Brief: From Survival to "Thrival"

I don't write this as an outsider or an academic. I write this as someone who spent the first 40 years of her life in narcissistic relationships.

I was raised by an adoptive mother who was drug-addicted and deeply self-absorbed. She mentally, emotionally, physically, and sexually abused me. At 17, I left home. By 18, I was married to a highly narcissistic man from a narcissistic cult who later kidnapped our son. I escaped after seven years. It took another two years of fighting and rebuilding to get my son back.

When I finally reached out for help and found people I could trust, my life began to change. With encouragement, mentoring, and a lot of inner work, I rebuilt myself.

I became co-Queensland Businesswoman of the Year in 1993, voted by the Women in Business Council. I was offered modelling work and found myself on film sets. I started a charity—Shambhallah Awareness Centre—on 168 acres of lush, healing rainforest in Tallebudgera Valley on the Gold Coast, to support and empower other women who had been victims of abuse.

I thought I had finally made it. I felt strong, successful, and independent.

And then I met the most dangerous narcissist of my life. Let's call him Tony.

Tony was charming, very intelligent, with an off the chart IQ. My attraction phenotype is sapiosexual: a person who finds intelligence sexually arousing. Add to this he was physically gorgeous— a heavyweight body builder, tanned, muscular, blonde, blue-eyed. When I was introduced to him by an anthropology professor from

Newcastle University, and he started flirting with me, I stopped thinking with my head; my hormones and my loneliness got in the way. He had a way of appearing innocent and naïve that made a person want to protect him. This facade was incredibly cunning. It was designed to trigger every nurturing impulse. If I had been thinking with my head, I would have easily seen he was just one explosion in a science lab away from being a comic-book evil-genius archetype. Yet, for two years we had a long-distance relationship, whilst my intuition kept whispering that something wasn't right.

When my long-term lease at Shambhallah ended, he insisted I move in with him. That meant shutting down everything I'd built on the Gold Coast and moving to Sydney, far away from my support network. Once I arrived, the isolation began. He persuaded me to spend my savings renovating his house. As soon as the work was finished, and he thought that i had no money left to move out if I need to, the mask came off and the full force of the narcissistic abuse began.

I stayed eight weeks.

The abuse escalated into physical violence. He was

three times my body weight. One assault left me with a minor skull fracture and internal injuries from being knocked down and kicked.

Incredibly, he tried to take me to court, claiming *I* had abused *him*. (A pattern that, I was to later find out, he repeated in many of his relationships.) The judge took one look at us both and dismissed his claims, throwing him out of the court room to protect my safety.

When I left hospital, I packed my things and walked away. He was shocked that I had the strength to go. But by this time, I had learned the power of reaching out. Friends in Sydney rallied around me, saw clearly what was happening, and helped me move and recover what I could. An old boss even flew from Melbourne to help me financially and support me as I rebuilt once again.

Within a year, I met my soulmate—the happiest relationship of my life. We've now been together for 22 years.

One year after meeting him, I was invited to star in a reality TV show called *The One*, which outrated *Baywatch* in Australia and was later sold overseas. From there, I launched several successful businesses, including a publishing company.

At 62, I find myself modelling again and working on film sets on the Gold Coast. My life didn't just recover—it blossomed.

Why This Workbook Exists

During the lockdowns, I received a message on Facebook from a woman named Jo-Ann Byers. She had been married to Tony for ten years after I left him.

Before I moved in with him, Tony had started seeing her. He also had a plan: he desperately wanted his name on a book. I was a journalist and suggested we create a book together—my writing, his editing. In truth, he contributed very little. His style was overly academic and not very communicative, but he was my partner and we were planning a future together. At the time, sharing the project made sense.

Jo-Ann was a book publisher, and Tony saw an opportunity. He stole the manuscript I had written and had it published under his name by her company.

After we separated, he fled to the United States to avoid criminal charges and married Jo-Ann. Ten years later, he did the same thing to her—stole her book and had it published elsewhere in his own interest.

During lockdown, after he had repeated his pattern with her, Jo-Ann reached out to me. She apologised, as she could now see that the lies he had told her about me were just that—lies. She realised she had been unknowingly seeing him behind my back and felt terrible about it.

She also discovered that, just as with her own story, the book she had once published for him had actually been my work.

Our conversations were healing for both of us. We could finally compare experiences and recognise the same patterns of manipulation, theft, and emotional abuse. We both realised the same thing:

A recovery workbook on narcissistic abuse needed to exist.

Not just a storybook, but a *practical guide* with clear steps to help people move through their own recovery—without being overwhelmed.

That is how this book was born.

Justice, Healing, and True "Revenge"

When you have been abused by a narcissist, it's natural to want justice. You want the world to see what they are, to acknowledge your pain, to side with you.

In an ideal world, people like Tony would be clearly identified early on. Their escalating narcissistic behaviours—often moving into criminal and sometimes life-threatening patterns—would be stopped before they destroy lives.

But we don't live in an ideal world. We live in a world with a *legal* system, not a true *justice* system. The courts can enforce laws, but they don't always deliver emotional justice. Many narcissistically abusive partners are never properly held accountable.

If you pour all your energy into chasing legal and moral justice, you can remain emotionally tied to the narcissist for years—long after they are physically gone.

Your healing is more important.

Talking with Jo-Ann helped both of us release a great deal of old pain. She told me that Tony had heard about my success in Australia and that it burned him. Narcissists often want their former partners to fail after leaving them, to "prove" they were the best thing that ever happened to you.

That is why my new intention is this:
To create a successful book—with Jo-Ann—that helps others heal from exactly the kind of abuse we survived. A book that will outshine anything he ever stole.

Because in the world of narcissistic abuse, the old saying really is true:

Success is the best revenge.

When you build a happy, healthy, successful life after the narcissist, you expose the lie that they were your saviour.

Instead, the truth becomes obvious: they were holding you back from everything you could be.

From Survival to "Thrival"

This little book is designed to help you move beyond survival into what I like to call **THRIVAL**—a life where you don't just exist, you *flourish*.

You don't need to know the whole path right now. You don't need to see the finish line. All you need is the willingness to take the **next three steps** laid out in these pages.

We'll take this slowly, in manageable pieces.

You will learn to understand what has happened to you, to reconnect with your own strength, and to begin rebuilding your life—on your terms, in your time.

So, let's begin.
Let's work through these steps together and get you on the road to your new, successful, thriving life.

Preface

This book is a collaboration between ancient tales and modern, between victims of both genders, between people from different countries and between myself and another woman who both suffered at the hands of the same narcissist!

Thank you to everyone who has had the courage to contribute to this work.

Narcissists triumph by keeping their victims in isolation.

Reading this book is only your first step.

You must reach out.

From personal experience, I can tell you that narcissists are good at tricking people into believing their side of the story. However, they don't fool everyone. Most people will have a feeling that something is not ringing true. Ask for help. Don't be ashamed to tell your story. People will help you. There are people who will believe you. Narcism can be overthrown only by reaching out for help and collaboration with others.

Above everything, this book is about your journey to freedom and recovery.

This Is a 'Victims of Narcissists' Recovery Work Book

Healing from Narcissistic abuse is a three-stage process:
1. Firstly, you need to realise that you are a victim, what sort of abuse you have suffered and how it has profoundly affected you.
2. Begin the process of recovery. The exercises in this book will help you begin this process.
3. Find help and support.

Recovery is an ongoing process. There are practical processes to help you move through these stages step by step. The ten steps in this book are designed to move you from victim consciousness to survivor then thriver. However, recovery from any abuse is an ongoing process. There is no end point at which you can say clearly that you have fully recovered. It is a journey of recovery. The yellow brick road doesn't end here, Dorothy; you can conquer the Emerald City. This book will take you down the path to becoming a recovering person who is no longer a victim and has decided to thrive in this world.

Work through these exercises in this book. Please don't skip any; do them in the order presented, as one leads into the next. The most crucial step for you is the current one. Each step leads to the next step. There is a logical step-by-step progression down the path of recovery, and there are no shortcuts. Don't worry about doing all of the steps. Don't overwhelm yourself. Just focus on your next step. Each step will lead you to complete your journey. You have to be determined to go the distance to survive.

These exercises can help you progress from being a:
- NAV (Narcissistic abuse victim)
- to a NAS (Narcissistic abuse survivor)
- And finally, a NAT (Narcissistic abuse thriver)

They are designed as a structured process of self-discovery and empowerment.

Jot down thoughts and make notes in the margins as you are reading this – this is your personal workbook. There is plenty of space in this book to write things.

You can **buy a special notebook as your personal Journal of Recovery**. It can be your companion to this text. In this, you can make notes of any thoughts that occur to you as you begin your process of self-examination. It will also provide extra space for you to give longer answers than the space provided here in the pages of this text.

NB: These exercises are not designed to diagnose any clinical conditions, and they are not to replace a skilled therapist who specialises in narcissistic abuse recovery.

Your therapist may want to work along with you in this workbook. That is fine if you are comfortable sharing your notes and results. You may want to keep the notes in this book private. That is also perfectly fine.

It is assumed that before you begin any of these workbook exercises, you have read through all of the previous parts of this book. I know you want to get right into it, but each part of this book builds on the previous. The information is delivered in an order that will aid your psyche's growth and develop your inner strength to move you to freedom. Remember: Don't skip over the stories of fellow former victims. They are essential.

You are not alone.

What Is Narcissism?

As a concept, narcissism has been around for centuries. Lately, the buzz around the term has grown louder, particularly about romantic relationships. But what exactly is narcissism?

At its core, narcissism is a form of extreme self-absorption. Narcissists are obsessed with themselves and their own needs and desires. They believe they are special and unique and that the world revolves around them. This sense of entitlement often leads to narcissistic behaviours, such as taking advantage of others, being excessively critical or judgmental, or demanding constant attention and admiration.

The term "narcissism" was first used by the British physician Havelock Ellis in 1898 to describe a psychological condition characterised by an "excessive love of one's self." In recent years, the term "narcissism" has been used more broadly to describe a range of self-absorbed behaviours or "Narcissistic Personality Disorders."

A Spectrum Of Narcissism

Narcissism exists on a continuum, from healthy narcissism to pathological narcissism. Healthy narcissism is characterised by a strong sense of self-worth and an ability to maintain healthy relationships. Pathological narcissism is characterised by an excessive need for admiration, a lack of empathy, and a sense of entitlement. People with pathological narcissism often have difficulty maintaining long-term relationships and may engage in manipulative or abusive behaviours.

The Diagnostic and Statistical Manual of Mental Disorders (DSM-5), the standard reference used by mental health professionals to diagnose mental disorders, categorises narcissism as a "personality disorder." The DSM-5 lists nine criteria for diagnosing narcissistic personality disorder, including:

- A grandiose sense of self-importance
- A preoccupation with fantasies of unlimited success, power, or beauty
- A belief that one is special and unique and can only be understood by other special or high-status people

- A need for excessive admiration
- A sense of entitlement
- A lack of empathy
- An interpersonally exploitative attitudes
- Envy of others or believing that others are envious of them
- Arrogance and haughty behaviours

As per the criteria, demonstration of five or more of the above is considered Narcissistic Personality Disorder. While a professional can diagnose it with clinical accuracy, you can get a sense of it if you display most of these qualities.

Narcissistic Personality Disorder

Individuals with narcissistic personality disorder (NPD) exhibit a lack of ability to empathise with others due to an inflated sense of self-importance, beauty, success or intelligence. Though people with this condition are frequently described as arrogant, self-centred, manipulative, and demanding, they are very often also abusers. Their grandiose fantasies allow them to see themselves as better than others. As such, they have no compunction in taking advantage of others to reach their own goals. Manipulation, gaslighting and abuse of those closest to them are standard, as they disregard the feelings of others, showing little or no respect or appreciation for any assistance rendered to them. They see people who help or enable them as useful, easily manipulated fools who deserve to be 'taken advantage of'. They see kindness as a weakness. They are interested in people only for how useful they are to them. When an individual's usefulness ends, the narcissist quickly becomes bored with them. Narcissists put all people down whilst trying to associate with people who are unique or gifted or elite, people they believe will enhance their status. This enhances their self-esteem, which is typically fragile underneath their arrogant bravado.

Modern movie media projects us into the role of the screen protagonist, which justifies his behaviour by the end result of him becoming the hero. For example, the modern mythic uber-man, James Bond, is sneaky and less ethical than his supervillains, and the passing parade of Bond women is simply a consumable product of his quest. Modern media is a modern myth that does not bring happiness to those who absorb the archetypes. Pat MacDonald, author of the paper "Narcissism in the Modern World," notes: *"We have a narcissistic society where self-promotion and individuality seem to be essential, yet in our hearts that's not what we want. We want to be part of a community, we want to be supported when we're struggling, we want a sense of belonging. Being extraordinary is not a necessary component to being loved."*

Ancient Greek myth tells of the consequence of falling in love with a narcissist or of the narcissist attempting to love. Narcissistic personality disorder derives its name from the myth retold by Ovid of Narcissus and Echo. It provides a timeless cautionary tale about the dangers of self-love and the perils of unrequited love. Though Narcissus and Echo's story is a tragedy, it can teach us a lot about what it means to be in a relationship with a narcissist. Narcissists are often charming and charismatic at first. They may sweep you off your feet with their grandiose gestures and their seeming dedication to making the relationship work. But over time, their true colours will start to show.

The abuse of a spouse is as old as time. It is sadly heartening to find accounts of this specific form of abuse in ancient myths and legends. Objections to it have been raised in morés of ancient cultures.

Before the advent of mass media, stories, myths and legends were seen as a way of changing the collective consciousness. Issues were depicted in allegory and justly dealt with by the fates. Human nature was challenged by the gods to either triumph or fail. Greek myth is beneficial. It highlights both the divinity and the foibles of human nature. It provoked reaction and healing. It stirred sympathy and outrage. The great myths have survived the test of time and lost little in the retelling due to the universality of their shared experience. Many have been retold and added to and yet have grown in popularity and thrived. They remind us that our love and pain are the shared experience of being human.'

Though we have more gadgets to amuse us in this modern age, when we bare our souls, we see our suffering shared through the millennia across race, code and creed as universal. The experience of being human has not changed since Ovid first collected all the popular myths from the known world and reset them to poetic meter in his classical work "Metamorphoses." i.e. 'The Hope of Transformation.' The mythmaker hopes that society will heed the warning in their tales and evolve, that the myth will become redundant when the moral is universally absorbed.

There are some myths from some cultures that feel alien to us. These are the ones that have completed their task. For example, the biblical myth of 'Lots Daughters' getting their father drunk enough to impregnate them is abhorrent by today's standards, not righteous. Incestuous drug rape is universally no longer acceptable under any circumstances, by any gender, in any culture. Yet, after all of this time and all the myths decrying violence against spouses, such as the troubadour tales, it is still seen as acceptable in modern media.

An example of this is spokespeople from the 'Me Too' movement claiming that Jonny Depp should have been found guilty, regardless of the proof of the abuse he suffered from his narcissistic spouse. Yet, we know that this does not feel right. There is an extreme lack of empathy and justice in these statements. These statements could cause that movement to be labelled as narcissistic and undo all the good that they have accomplished. Wanting a man who has been proven innocent in a court of law to be found guilty to advance the agenda of a cause has all the hallmarks of NPD.

Some experts say that we live in an age of narcissism, where people are more focused on themselves than others. Is this because modern culture is collectively becoming increasingly narcissistic?

Narcissism in the Modern Age

There is no single "cause" of narcissism. Some experts believe that narcissism is the result of early childhood development. Others believe that it is a combination of genetic and environmental factors.

An upbringing that involves pampering, overindulgence, or excessively high expectations that contribute to the development of narcissistic tendencies. A parent who is overly critical or demands perfection from a child can also foster narcissistic behaviours.

In some cases, narcissism may be the result of a traumatic event, such as abuse or neglect. Children who are exposed to trauma often have difficulty forming attachments and may become disconnected from their emotions. This emotional numbness can lead to a sense of grandiosity and a need for admiration as they seek to fill the "emotional void" with outside approval.

Environmental factors are not the only ones that can influence the development of narcissism. There is also a strong genetic component. Studies have shown that narcissism runs in families and that it has a high heritability. This means that if you have a parent or close relative who is a narcissist, you are more likely to develop narcissistic tendencies yourself.

Some scientists have documented that narcissists suffer from decreased grey matter in specific centres of the brain. This creates biological brain damage, rendering them incapable of sophisticated emotions such as trust, love, intimacy, compassion, empathy, vulnerability, sincerity, or remorse. This leaves them neurologically predisposed to callousness, impulsivity and addiction.

The Different Types Of Narcissists

Not all narcissists are the same. There are three different types of narcissists, each with its own set of behaviours and traits:

(1) The grandiose narcissist: This type of narcissist is characterised by an inflated sense of self-importance, a need for admiration, and a lack of empathy. Grandiose narcissists often seek out high-status or influential people to boost their egos. They may also engage in risky or impulsive behaviours to feel more alive.

(2) The vulnerable narcissist: This type of narcissist is characterised by feelings of insecurity and a need for reassurance. Vulnerable narcissists often have difficulty handling criticism or setbacks and may react with anger or hostility. They may also withdraw from people or activities to protect themselves from further hurt.

(3) The malignant narcissist: This type of narcissist is characterised by a sense of grandiosity, a lack of empathy, and a desire to control or manipulate others. Malignant narcissists are often paranoid and may engage in aggressive or even violent behaviours. They may also try to undermine or destroy the relationships of those around them to feel superior.

The different types of narcissism can help us understand the different behaviours that narcissists display. However, it is essential to remember that narcissism exists on a continuum, and not all narcissists will display all of the behaviours mentioned above.

Your Relationship with a Narcissist

The charm of a narcissist can be hard to resist. They are very good at disguising their true intentions and can be extremely convincing when they want something from you. Narcissists are self-absorbed, selfish, and arrogant. Despite these behaviours, they crave attention and admiration and often use manipulation or coercion to get it.

Narcissists need validation as they secretly reject themselves. They feel they have no true identity, becoming human chameleons. Never being taught how to interact with others correctly, when they need to fit in, they will take on a fake persona. They create false egos and false aggrandising stories about themselves in their mind. They begin to project these out to the people around them, feeling that the people who accept these fictions are fools; the irony is that they need other's acceptance of the false grandiose stories they have manufactured to validate themselves.

In Greek, the word persona means 'mask.' Narcissists are very good at wearing masks. They will use different personas for different occasions. They will mimic the character and emotions of those around them. They fail to see the value in emotions, so they can only temporarily mimic them. As with a mask, there is nothing behind their eyes. A narcissist can shape-shift into the people they've abused, stealing their identities. Not that all people do it intentionally, but narcissists take advantage of others to get what they want. It is not just all about attention. Narcissists feel they have a right to get everything they want, regardless of the physical, emotional, or financial cost to others.

Yet, in this scenario, the potential victim must remember that they hold all the power, as when they remove their attention without validation, the narcissist becomes nothing. Their illusionary construct topples. Once you see them for what they are, all that remains is a fragile creature, their true self.

While it is possible to have a healthy relationship with a mild narcissist, it is crucial to be aware of the potential pitfalls. The first consideration is the recognition of the signs that you may be dating a narcissist. It is essential to remember that not all narcissists will display all of the signs all of the time and that some people may exhibit some of these signs without being full-blown narcissists. Recognising the signs gives you the power to choose what you will consciously and won't tolerate. Additionally, it allows you to utilise techniques that may counter some narcissistic manipulations.

Identifying The Narcissistic Relationship

The most important thing that you must do, without a doubt, is identify the relationship as being a genuine narcissistic relationship. Many women are in doubt of this. The most common thing I hear from women who have been in a narcissistic relationship is them taking the blame. Their partner has convinced them for so long that it is them, not the narcissist, who is the problem. This is called gaslighting. And he is the classic warning sign that you are in a narcissistic relationship. The problem is the narcissist, not you. I am here to tell you: "No, it is not you. It IS them."

Take a nice, big red pencil and underline all of the following that apply to the partner that you were with. The following nine signs could indicate that you are dating a narcissist:

The Fairy-Tale Start

It all starts so well. They are charming and attentive, and you feel like the luckiest person in the world. They sweep you off your feet with grand gestures and promises of a future together. It feels too good to be true... because it is.

The narcissist gives just enough of what you want to keep you hooked. This is what is known as "love bombing." The pedestal phase is when the narcissist puts you up on a pedestal and idealises you. They make you feel like you are perfect and can do no wrong. This is usually when they try to win you over and get you to commit to them.

Conversation Hogging

Narcissists love to talk about themselves. They will monopolise the conversation and leave you feeling like you don't exist. They are the centre of their universe and expect you to revolve around them. A typical conversation would revolve around their accomplishments, their problems, and their day.

The Cravings for Compliments

Narcissists are constantly seeking validation and approval. They need to be the centre of attention and crave compliments. They will often fish for compliments or information about you, which they can use to make themselves look good. The inflated ego needs constant stroking, and they will do whatever it takes to get it.

A Lack of Empathy

Narcissists lack empathy, which means they are not able to understand or share the feelings of others. This lack of empathy is one of the most damaging aspects of narcissism. It can lead to a complete disregard for the rights and feelings of others.

Narcissists are often very selfish and only care about their own needs and wants. They have difficulty seeing things from another person's perspective and often only think about themselves.

Unreasonable Expectations

Narcissists often have unrealistic expectations of others. They may expect you to always be available for them or to drop everything for them at a moment's notice. They may also expect you to always agree with them and to do things their way. These unreasonable expectations can be very demanding and draining.

A Need for Control

Narcissists often need to control everything around them. They may try to control how you spend your time, who you spend it with, what you wear, what you eat, etc. They may also try to control your emotions and manipulate you into doing things their way. A narcissist's need for control often comes from a place of insecurity. They need to feel like they are in charge and in control of everything in their lives.

Lack of Meaningful Long-Term Friendships or Relationships

Narcissists often lack meaningful long-term friendships or relationships. They may have many acquaintances but usually don't have many close friends. This is because narcissists are often very self-centred and only care about themselves. They may use people to get what they want and discard them when they are no longer useful.

Gaslighting

Gaslighting is a form of emotional abuse where the narcissist tries to make you doubt your memories, perceptions, and sanity. They may do this by denying things you know to be true, making you feel like you are overreacting, or questioning your judgment. This can be a very confusing and frustrating experience. Gaslighting can make you doubt yourself and your reality.

Gaslighting can also be external. Where rumours and incredulous stories are spread about you to make others doubt your character and your sanity

Aggressiveness at Hearing a No

Narcissists often have a hard time hearing the word "no." They may become angry or aggressive when they don't get their way. This is because they are used to getting what they want and expect others to give in to their demands. Narcissists also have a hard time taking criticism. They may lash out at you if you point out their flaws or shortcomings.

These are just some of the symptoms of being in a relationship with a narcissist. If you are in a relationship with someone who exhibits these behaviours, it is vital to start considering what you're willing to tolerate and what you want for your future.

Survival Technique 1

Identifying Your Abuser as a Potential Narcissist

Do you have someone in your life, spouse, business partner or boss who is difficult to deal with? Being a problematic person does not necessarily mean that they are a narcissist. However, if they have a cluster of signifying behaviours, then we are starting to see what their patterns reveal about them more clearly. Clarity is a solid first step toward being able to make changes for the better.

Please score the following workbook questions on a scale from 1-10.
Remember: We are all on the narcissism spectrum somewhere. This quiz will help you determine if your partner suffers from the disordered end of the narcissistic personality spectrum.

One-Sided Listening

A Narcissist will adopt a tone of contempt for the other in their conversations. The most oft-quoted line for determining if you are dealing with a Narcissist is "Narcissistic listening dismisses, negates, ignores, minimises, denigrates or otherwise renders irrelevant other people's concerns and comments." The favoured opening for a reply remark by a narcissist is: *"But.."* They use it as a delete key to erase others' viewpoints from the discussion and negate whatever comments came before,

1. When discussing things with your partner, is what they have to say all that matters when you talk with them? Yes/No ___
2. Do they give you the feeling that conversations are all about what they want? Yes/No ___
3. When there are decisions to be made, are your concerns dismissed as irrelevant or inconvenient? Yes/No ___
4. If you expect to have input, you are undermining them? Yes/No ___
5. Are their opinions always right and yours always wrong or of little importance? ___

One-Sided Vision

For a narcissist, it is all about them. They are quite literally all they can see.

1. Is your partner always saying:" I know more. Or "I know better." Yes/No ___
2. Do they act like they are the most interesting person in the room? Yes/No ___

3. Do they take up most of the air time in conversations? Yes/No ___
4. Are they always talking about what they have done or their thoughts on a topic without asking you or others for an opinion? Yes/No ___
5. If you/someone else starts to talk about themselves, does your partner link back to things in their own life to focus the discussion back on them again? Yes/No ___
6. When they want something, they never ask you about it; they get it and don't even consider asking how you feel about it. Yes/No ___
7. Do they treat you like you are merely here to do things for them? Yes/No ___

NRA - No Rules Apply

Narcissists experience themselves above others, so they feel rules don't apply to them.

1. Does your partner break social and moral codes without concern for how their actions may affect others? Yes/No ___
2. Do they have affairs? Yes/No ___

3. Do they push into queues in front of other waiting people? Yes/No ___
4. Do they cheat on their Taxes? Yes/No ___
5. Do they generally ignore any rules that get in the way of their doing what they want? Yes/No ___
6. Do they say:" Rules are for other people to follow?" Yes/No ___

Super-Sensitivity to Criticisms

The paradox of narcissism is that they can simultaneously hold an inflated idea of their importance and be deflated by negative feedback. They criticise others, but they see any criticism as a personal attack. The clinical term for taking others' concerns as personal criticism is personalising. *"I'm feeling lonely,"* gets heard by someone narcissistic as the accusation: *"You don't spend enough time with me."*

1. Does your partner go on the attack when you criticise them? Yes/No ___
2. Do they try to hurt you back for the perceived hurt of criticism? Yes/No ___

3. If you say you are unhappy about anything, does your partner think you are criticising them? Yes/No ___

4. When your partner hears others talk about personal feelings, do they believe it is a veiled criticism of themselves? Yes/No ___

5. If you are expressing negative feelings, for example, engendered by work or with people that have nothing to do with them, do they interpret your negative feelings as indirect criticism of them? Yes/No ___

Blaming Others

Narcissists feel safer blaming and fault-finding in others rather than accepting responsibility for their part in difficulties. This prevents personal growth.

1. Does your partner refuse to apologise when they are in the wrong? Yes/No ___

2. Do they feel they are above others and reproach? Yes/No ___

3. If you ask them how they feel, do they react as if they think you are saying that they have contributed to a problem? Yes/No ___

4. Do they get explosively mad at you? Yes/No ___
5. Do they exhibit all-or-nothing thinking? i.e. "If they've done one thing that's not right, then they must be all bad."Yes/No ___

Lack of Appreciation

Blaming others and not listening and seeing what your partner has done quickly result in a lack of appreciation and gratitude.

1. Does your partner express appreciation for the things you do for them? Yes/No ___
2. Do they use manners when addressing you? Yes/No ___
3. When you do something for your partner, do they make you feel like it's not good enough or you have not done enough? Yes/No ___
4. If you give them a gift, do they refuse to open it or cast it aside casually without comment? Yes/No ___
5. If you give them a gift, do they make you feel like you got them the wrong thing? Yes/No ___

Quick to Anger and Anger is Blamed on Your Actions . . .

Narcissists display public social charm. Privately, they are a very different person. Narcissists are quick to anger and blame their anger on others, usually the safe targets of those closest to them.

Does your partner frequently say any of the following phrases or words to that effect?...

1. "You made me mad. Yes/No ___
2. You didn't listen to me. Yes/No ___
3. You criticised me. Yes/No___
4. You're trying to control me. Yes/No ___
5. Your view is wrong. Yes/No ___
6. So YOU need to apologise, not me. Yes/No___
7. If I'm mad, it's because I'm frustrated by what you are doing. Yes/No___
8. I'm only mad because you ... " Yes/No ___

TOTAL SCORE: ___

What does this score indicate?

Scores of 50 or less indicate a healthy to average range.

A total score higher than 100-410, and there is a problem: the higher the score, the more help you may need.

Note that these score interpretations are based on general patterns.
They are not a clinical diagnosis.

Self-Blame and Self-Doubt

The Encyclopedia Britannica defines narcissistic *"Gaslighting" as "an elaborate and insidious technique of deception and psychological manipulation, usually practised by a single deceiver, or "gaslighter," on a single victim over an extended period."* The term is derived from the title of a 1944 movie, "Gaslight", starring Charles Boyer and Ingrid Bergman. After the death of her famous opera-singing aunt, Paula (Ingrid Bergman) is sent to study in Italy to become a great opera singer as well. While there, she falls in love with the charming Gregory Anton (Charles Boyer). The two return to London to live in her aunt's home, which Paula has inherited. Paula begins to become suspicious. However, Gregory, who is, in reality, a jewel thief and the murderer of Paula's aunt, convinces Paula that she's imagining things. To reinforce it, he attempts to convince her she is going insane. She notices missing pictures, strange footsteps, mysterious late-night appointments and gaslights that dim without being touched. Yet, Gregory tells her that she must be going mad. As she fights to retain her sanity, Scotland Yard inspector and former lover of her aunt, Brian

Cameron (Joseph Cotten), becomes suspicious of Gregory and sympathetic to Paula's plight and helps her to survive this narcissistic abuse.

Julia Roberts stars in a limited television series called "Gaslit." It tells the true story of Martha Mitchell (Julia Roberts), the wife of ex-US Attorney General John Mitchell (Sean Penn), during the Watergate scandal. Nixon operatives feared that if she learned of the false arrests of her husband's colleagues, she would begin talking to the press about possible assassinations ordered by the president. Martha Mitchell began to take her story public, but she was threatened, drugged and kidnapped. When released, few believed her. *"I'm a political prisoner. I'm black and blue,"* she told reporter Helen Thomas. When she began to talk about Watergate, her stories and thoughts were often not treated as serious news. The Nixon administration began to counter by discrediting her, "spreading rumours that she was an alcoholic suffering from mental illness," in the Washington Post. Narcissistic abuse by the government.

The narcissist will never want to be wrong. They will try to convince you that you are always the one in the wrong by making you doubt your memories, perceptions, and sanity. This process of Gaslighting can include denying things that you know to be true, making you feel like you are overreacting, or making you question your judgment. You can begin to doubt yourself and your reality.

Abusers convince victims that the abuser's poor behaviour is their fault. Then emotional abuse becomes physical abuse, and the layering of abuses begins to build. Narcissistic emotional abuse that produces self-blame keeps the victim in a relationship that continues to get more abusive. The more complex the layers of abuse, the more symptoms of Complex PTSD can result.

The abuser learns how far to take it, beginning slowly and escalating the abuse over time. Abusers want their 'whipping boy' to stay, so they become experts in slowly turning up the volume to gradualise the victim. Gradualism is described as the process of heating water slowly so that the frog won't jump out of the cooking pot. The first act of emotional abuse in a relationship may be as simple as a rude comment. The abuser then gages their next attack based on how the victim responds to the previous attack. If the victim ignores the comment or, worse, makes excuses for it, then the abuser knows they can get away with more. Just like a bratish child, the abuser will keep testing their limits. If a person puts up with the lesser abuses, then they have just taught the abuser that they are willing to be victimised. If the victim stays in the abusive relationship, the occurrences and levels of abuse WILL increase over time.

In a similar way that terrorists create Stockholm syndrome in their captives, a new interpersonal view is created in the relationship by the abuser. To do this, the relationship expectations of the victim are managed down by the abuser to the point the abuser does not have to give any nourishing input. The abuser creates financial dependency, where the victims may be dependent on the abuser for the necessities of life, or an emotional addiction, where the victim craves any attention, even if it is negative, or both. In some instances, the abuser becomes the enabler for a physical addiction, or conversely, the person with an addiction manages its victims to become the enabler. Additionally, the abuser gives the victim false hope of an improvement in the relationship in the future. *"He will behave better when he gets that promotion", "...when his son speaks to him again," "...when he's not so depressed."* etc. Every victim speaks of the moments of flashes of decent behaviour towards them like a holy grail. This causes intermittent reinforcement, which becomes less and less over time.

Survival Technique 2

Gaslighting Gauge

Do any of the following apply in your relationship:

1. Is your partner insisting things are different to the way you remember them? Yes / No
2. Do you doubt that you are right about something you know you are right about if your partner insists it is different? Yes / No ___
3. Do you think that your memory must be getting bad? Yes / No ___
4. Do you find that you give in to your partner when you know you are right? Yes / No
5. Is it just too much effort to insist that a fact is so, as it will be pointless and not change anything? Yes / No ___

6. Do you have negative, strong gut feelings about your partner's behaviour, but they convince you that you are mistaken? Yes / No ___
7. Do you doubt your intuition now when your intuition was spot on before this relationship? Yes / No ___
8. Do you find yourself asking your partner what they want to do, as it will be pointless to try to do anything else? Yes / No ___

If you answered yes to any of these questions, please rate them on a scale of 1- 10 regarding how frequently they occur - 1 being hardly ever and 10 being always. If your score is between 11 and 80, you must start believing yourself and expecting others to do so.

Note that these score interpretations are self-examinations. They are not a clinical diagnosis.

Consciously Countering Self-Doubt

Rather than giving in, or giving up, or doubting yourself, try this:

Where you know you are right, try finishing a disagreement with: *"Well, that is MY opinion."* and leave it at that! Do not be drawn into any further discussion on the topic. Walk away, leave the room or even go out for a while. Just finish with that statement. Then, be silent. Don't be drawn back into conversation.

Your opinion is yours, and you are entitled to your own opinions. They are your personal beliefs and are not wrong because they are yours and no one else's. If a narcissist is trying to gaslight you, your opinion is your final word on the matter.

The narcissist will have put a lot of effort into setting up this dispute to prove you wrong for their purposes, so don't participate in it.

Stay silent on this topic. Don't be drawn back into conversation. If they try to bring the topic up again later, they immediately shut it down again. Just say, *"Well, that is MY opinion."* again. Then, be silent. Don't feed them more energy on the disputed topic; otherwise, you reward their bad behaviour.

This can start you on the road back to self-belief.

Who Was Narcissus?

The term Narcissist is derived from a personal name, Narcissus. Many modern many mental disorders , including this psychopathy, derive names from Greek mythic archetypes.

In a nutshell, Narcissus was a handsome young man who fell in love with his own reflection. Echo, a mountain nymph, loved Narcissus and followed him everywhere. When Narcissus realised that Echo loved him, he rejected her. When Narcissus died, Echo mourned over the body until she, too, faded away.

Just like Echo, you may find yourself in a relationship with a narcissist. And just like Echo, you may find yourself feeling trapped, confused, and exhausted. If you're in a relationship with a narcissist, you may feel like you're walking on eggshells all the time, never quite sure what will set them off. You may feel like you're always trying to please them and never quite measuring up.

In the Latin myth, Narcissus was the son of the River God Cephisus and the nymph Lyriope. Narcissus' parents were worried because of the extraordinary beauty of their baby. They asked the blind prophet Teiresias about their son's future. Tiresias was Apollo's most prominent prophet on earth. He was the oldest living human; he had been a woman and given birth; he had been dead, had offended some of the gods, and had been blessed by others. Teiresias mediated between humankind and the gods, male and female, blind and seeing, present and future, this world and the underworld. Teiresias had learned in his long life that some people do not want to hear the whole answer to what they asked. So he cryptically told the concerned parents that the boy would grow old only if "he did not get to know himself".

However, by the time he was 15 years of age, Narcissus was very self-absorbed. "Himself" was all that mattered to himself. Narcissus became famous for his extraordinary beauty, and he was a particular favourite of the Sun God Apollo due to his extraordinary physique. Soon, he became arrogant and vain, rudely rejecting every little bit of attention he received from men and women. A young man named Aminias fell in love with

Narcissus but was particularly rudely rejected. Heartless Narcissus gave Aminias a sword to kill himself so he would no longer be a problem. Shattered, distressed and confused, the youth Aminias committed suicide at Narcissus' doorstep, praying to the Gods to give Narcissus a lesson in empathy for all the pain he had thoughtlessly provoked in others. Aminias' spirit became an avenging daemon. Nemesis, the Goddess of Revenge, heard the story from Aminias' daemon and decided to punish Narcissus.

On his 16th birthday, Narcissus walked into the deep forest away from all his admirers. He walked far and became thirsty, so he decided to drink some water from a nearby crystal clear lake. In the water, he saw the most beautiful creature he had ever seen. He tried to talk to it. Yet, like he had done to many, it refused to talk back to him. He reached his hand out to the creature in the water, but the water wavered at his touch, and he could no longer see the image of the beautiful one. He panicked. "Come back. Come back." He cried in distress. He had never felt loss or disappointment before. He had always been given everything he wanted, and this he wanted more than anything he had ever desired. Finally, he realised it was his own reflection in the water, yet he could not bring himself to drink for fear of destroying the image. He remained entranced by the reflection of himself in the water, forgetting to drink to slake his thirst. He pined as so many had done when they had looked at him and could not obtain the object of their desire. Others had given up, but Narcissus always had gotten what he wanted and did not know how to face his disappointment. He tried to keep looking at the beautiful reflection. There, he remained motionless at the banks of the crystal lake, stubbornly refusing to drink and staring at the beautiful image of himself in sorrow. Did Narcissus gain empathy for Aminias's plight before he died of thirst? Apparently not. According to the myth, Narcissus is still admiring himself in the underworld, still suffering from an endless thirst as he stares at his reflection, looking up at him from the waters of the river Styx.

By falling in love with his reflection, Narcissus received the punishment that he deserved for his lack of empathy in the treatment of others. He also exposed the love of beauty and of the other as the love of self, leading to self-knowledge, self-completion, and self-fulfilment. But have we lost balance with this self-love today?

Immaturity and Rehabilitation

This mythic story implies that narcissism is a youthful folly, a maturity issue. However, the modern epidemic is an adult concern. Grijalva et al.'s epidemiological meta-analysis of the condition in 2015 revealed some frightening statistics. Mature prevalence of NPD is estimated as high as 6% in the general population, rising as high as 16% in clinical populations. Less than 3% of those diagnosed with Narcissistic Personality Disorder ever 'grow out of it.' Just as, in allegorical terms, Narcissus himself carried the condition through into his afterlife, so too modern narcissists find rehabilitation nearly impossible. Added to this is that modern culture rewards and idolises so many narcissists in real life. The media tells us that 'the US president achieved his goal through narcissism, not through a desire to serve.' Gordon Gekko tells us that "Greed is good." Even our new-age spiritual movements have taken up the cry of "Me, me, ME!"

At one end of the self-loving spectrum is the charismatic leader with an excess of charm, whose only vice may be their inflated amour-propre. At the opposing end of the spectrum reside individuals with full-blown narcissistic personality disorder, whose grandiosity soars to such heights that they are manipulative and easily angered, especially when they don't receive the attention they consider their birthright. Additionally, those exhibiting NPD are not always rude and unpleasant, which can make it hard to see where they sit in the spectrum initially. Narcissistic folks can be delightful to hang out with. They cut a larger-than-life figure through the world. They know how to be charming, are good at things, and present the perfect politically correct appearance in public. On the negative end, this is solely to generate the maximum emotive effect from the simple creatures they desire something from. They can be consummate performers, portraying themselves as compassionate and generous when, in truth, they are not. Superficially, they often look like they would be desirable as friends and even as marriage partners. The desire to sustain a friendship, never mind a love relationship, can quickly fade with someone who does not seem to see or hear you, who dismissively pushes away what you say.

Listening is an act of love for the other. Love is about listening and really hearing and understanding. It takes time and a desire to understand the other. It requires putting the effort into listening to them. Narcissistic functioning, at its core, is a disorder of listening. A narcissist only listens to themselves. Think of it as one-sided listening. A partner who changes the topic and gets defensive or gets mad at you when you try to talk about difficulties you've been experiencing is not a good choice for a life partner. These are symptoms of mid-spectrum NPD. If they are quick to anger, if you attempt to express your viewpoint, then you are heading down a dark path. This usually accelerates along a pattern into the far more dangerous behaviours of the malignant narcissist. The malignant narcissist is diagnosed as being sadistic, guiltless, remorseless, calculating, ruthless, inhumane, callous, brutal, aggressive, merciless, vicious, cruel, spiteful, hateful and jealous. They are paranoid, anticipating betrayal and seeking to punish. They are potentially suicidal or homicidal. A lack of willingness to listen can be an early warning sign for people wishing to avoid an abusive narcissistic partner.

Yes, though there are abused men, the statistics for the abuse of women are highly disproportionate to those of abused men. I love the beautiful, caring men in this world, and I am sad for those of you who have been victims of spousal abuse. Still, we have to acknowledge the increased abuse of women in an increasingly narcissistic society. The statistics show that this is an overwhelmingly gender-biased problem. 98% of all abused spouses are in heterosexual relationships. 97% of severely abused spouses are female. Psychology Today tells us that 75% of people diagnosed with Narcissistic Personality Disorder are male and 25% are female. Therefore, women should also appreciate that whilst it is an overwhelmingly female problem, it is not an exclusively female problem. Some estimates are as high as 30% of males, in either heterosexual or same-sex couples, are in abusive or severely abusive relationships. However, the rules for freeing yourself from narcissistic victimisation apply regardless of gender.

The epidemic is growing, spreading like a cancer, hiding like the elephant in the room. Its story needs to be told. It needs to be mythologised so that it can be eulogised. Once thoroughly examined and the collective psyche calls it unacceptable and repugnant, the myth will have lost its power as society evolves beyond impotent acknowledgement. Where are the movies in the media that will shock and make villains of abusive narcissists? Farrah Fawcett's shocking 1984 movie " The Burning Bed" comes to mind; its disturbing images made us cringe. The lack of acknowledgement of her plight in the legal system made us look away. The movie won awards, but they didn't tell more of these stories. Yet, now, we need to look and see more than ever. That is the style of the new myth that is necessary. Tell these stories until we can say, as a society, "I really can't relate to a culture of abuse. It is so strange that anybody would have ever let things like that happen."

Over 2000 years have passed since Ovid retold the story of Narcissus and Echo, and it is alarming that it is still so relevant today. But we can change this. We can change this in one generation or less, but we must examine the stories in all their horror; we cannot water them down with political correctness or gender equanimity. We must look and listen to the stories until they sicken us and move us to action. If we are unwilling to listen to these stories or are unempathetic to the plight of the victims, if we feel nothing and are more interested in me me me, than the suffering of other humans, then we have already gone down the dark path of the narcissist.

Who Was Echo?

Echo's Story is the story of the first woman ever to fall victim to a narcissist. Well, to THE Narcissus, to be exact. Her name was Echo. While we are being exact, I have to mention that she wasn't actually a woman either, yet that doesn't make her pain any less real. Echo was a wild woodland nymph. She lived in a pristine sylvan forest beside a crystal clear lake. Echo had the most beautiful voice in the world. She would sit in a naturally occurring amphitheatre behind the lake and sing. Her harmonic tones were amplified outwards by the shape of the rocks, carried across the water and would ring through the cedars. The animals of the forest were soothed and entranced by her singing. Echo also learned to be an excellent mimic. She learned to copy the calls of all the forest animals exactly. She could make the sounds of the brooks that babbled into the lake and the breeze that whispered through the trees. Echo was also a chronic helper. She could not stand to see anything in pain and would feel compelled to do everything she could to ease the suffering of another. She was kind to all the forest animals. She would help the sick or those wounded by the huntsman's bow.

The wounded animals she saw made her afraid of the human realm. Kings and princes would arrange hunting trips to her forest so they might have the luck to hear the magical music of her song. Being such a natural mimic, Echo quickly learned to copy human speech and sounds. If the wanderers in her forest heard her song or mimicry, their human hearts would also become entranced, just like the forest's creatures. All who heard her would search for her to make her their wife. Yet, she rejected all suitors, humans and gods, satyrs or fauns. Her lack of desire for a lover won her the admiration of the great Artemis, the virgin goddess of the moon, the hunt and all wild things.

The only thing that Artemis did not approve of was Echo's assistance to her father, Zeus, king of the gods. When he fought with Hera, his wife and queen of the gods, Zeus would hide from the fight in the magical forest. There, he could rest and meditate and clear his thoughts. However, if Hera was angry enough, she would come down after him, and Zeus would find no peace that day. There was only one thing that Hera and Zeus ever fought about: Zeus's many indiscretions. All the other gods believed Zeus deserved the occasional scalding from his wife for this.

But Echo felt pity for Zeus. Echo loved to help things in distress. So when she spotted Hera in the forest, Echo distracted her with her musical voice and then repeated every bit of gossip she could think of to sidetrack her attention away from searching for her miscreant husband. This worked well for some time, as Hera loved to gossip. When Hera realised why Echo was being her gossip buddy, Hera felt doubly betrayed—betrayed by Zeus and her newfound friend. So Hera punished Echo for being a perpetual gossip by limiting her voice to repeating the last few sounds she heard. Artemis refused to advocate for Echo or help her in any way, so the forest stopped ringing with the sounds of her music and became haunted by ghostly repeating sounds.

Echo and Narcissus

Echo happened to chance across Narcissus whilst he was lying on the bank of the crystal clear lake, hopelessly in love with his reflection. She heard him cry out: "Come back. Come Back." She felt his pain, and though she could not understand it, she was determined to help.

She came up beside him and repeated: "Come back. Come Back." in exactly Narcissus' voice. Narcissus looked around, startled. That was the most beautiful voice he had ever heard. He knew it must be the voice of the reflection. Echo hid herself.

"Who's there?" called Narcissus.

"Who's there?" answered Echo.

Narcissus stood up and ran toward the sound. "Come back," he called after the voice.

Echo turned and ran. "Come back," she called back to him.

"Come back," called Narcissus again.

"Come back," answered Echo. She hid in the bushes. No one spoke. The beautiful youth passed by her, and she saw his face entirely for the first time. His beauty struck her. She tried to sneak up on him from behind and embrace him. As she snuck towards him, she reminded herself she was also gorgeous, talented, and beloved of the gods. Indeed, this is the one that she had been saving herself for. She put her arms around him, and for a moment, Narcissus thought the beloved creature he had seen in the lake was embracing him. He turned slowly in her arms, expecting the lips, the eyes and face from his reflection. He was so disappointed to see such a lesser creature embracing him. He jumped back in disgust. Narcissus started and pushed her away. He was used to rejecting people and gods. What did he care about a wild wood nymph?

"Go away." He cried.

Echo tried to tell him he was loved and should drink something. Yet all that came out was, "Go away."

Narcissus was startled to hear his own voice come out of her mouth. "What is this?"

"What is this?" Echoed back.

"Why are you repeating what I say?" asked Narcissus

"Why are you repeating what I say?" repeated Echo

"Stop it and go away!" demanded Narcissus

"Stop it and go away!" repeated Echo helplessly

Narcissus turned without another word and fled back to his spot on the shores of the crystal lake. He was relieved to see his beautiful creature was still there. He waved at it, and at precisely that moment, it waved back at him. Suspicious, he moved his head from side to side. The creature in the lake's water mimicked his actions. He glanced up at Echo hovering beside him. No. It wasn't her. Then he noticed her reflection over the shoulder of his lake creature. He looked up at her and back at the water. He realised he was looking at his own reflection. He burst into mournful wails. It was the only beautiful and perfect thing in the world, and he could not have it. Echo tried to comfort him, but he pushed her away violently. He dashed his hand into his reflection. As soon as he had done so, he regretted it. The ripples in the water distorted his reflection. He was consumed with an overwhelming feeling of loss and horror when he could no longer see his reflection. He sat still and quiet until the stillness returned to the water, and with it returned the vision of the only thing he had ever loved. He was relieved. He would not take his eyes from it again. He was fascinated, transfixed, hypnotised. Was this him? Was this the feeling he inspired in others? Just then, he was inspiring pity in Echo. She gathered sweet and juicy fruits to help slake his thirst. He threw them at her, resenting that she had made him look away from himself for an instant.

She fauned over him, and he yelled at her: "I want you out of the picture."

"I want you out of the picture." Echo returned.

This is useless, he thought. "You are stupid as well as annoying."

Heartbroken, with tears in her eyes, Echo reflected his words back to him: "You are stupid as well as annoying."

Narcissus did not care about her tears. She was a waste of space and fresh air. He wanted her gone to have his moment with his beloved self. "Get away from me, you freak."

"Get away from me, you freak."

But what if he should need something? Narcissus thought he should keep this idiot close just in case. Without saying a word, he looked up at her with puppy dog sad eyes. Echo rushed towards him.

"Not so close, you idiot. Just stay over there."

Echo's legs gave way under her, and she collapsed where she was. "Not so close, you idiot. Just stay over there." Narcissus smiled at her, and there she stayed.

Echo ignored the insults and made excuses for Narcissus. 'He is stressed, tired, and thirsty. He would not normally be like this.' She reasoned to herself. In truth, she had no idea what he was like typically. However, Echo thought she had almost distracted him enough to drink. The harder Echo tried, the more violent Narcissus became with her. The more violent he became, the more Echo could see that he was on the path of destruction, so she tried to help more. From the outside, it is easy to see this was a no-win situation for both parties. There were only two outcomes. What would happen first? Would Narcissus commit suicide from dehydration first, or would he kill Echo out of his frustration before he passed over?

Narcissus weakened quickly from dehydration, being only human, not divine as he thought. He used all of the last of his strength, struggling to keep his eyes open. Indeed, he died with his eyes wide open, lost in his fascination with himself. The Sun god, Apollo, took pity on him, and he sprang up alive again as the purple Narcissus flower or purple daffodil, short-lived but one of the most beautiful flowers in the world. This represents the hope that in the next life, Narcissus will flourish.

Artemis returned to the scene to see if vengeance had taken place as Nemesis and Hera wanted. In his novel "The Alchemist," Paolo Coehlo invents a report of Artemis on the account of Narcissus in which he suggests that after Narcissus died, the goddess of the forest, Artemis, appeared and found the lake of fresh water transformed into a lake of salty tears.

"'Why do you weep?' the Goddess asked.

'I weep for Narcissus,' the lake replied.

'Ah, it is no surprise that you weep for Narcissus,' ... you alone could contemplate his beauty close at hand.'

'But... was Narcissus beautiful?' the lake asked.

'Who better than you to know that?' the Goddess said in wonder, 'After all, it was by your banks that he knelt ... to contemplate himself!'

The lake was silent for some time. Finally, it said: 'I weep for Narcissus, but I never noticed that Narcissus was beautiful. I weep because, each time he knelt beside my banks, I could see in the depths of his eyes, my beauty reflected."

The illusion or possibility of love is often what the good person devotes themselves to in a narcissistic relationship. You may find yourself making excuses for them or saying:

> "They are really a good person deep down."
> "I know this relationship could be great if we could only return to how we were before."
> "I can help them change, and then this relationship will reach its full potential."

> *"They are only treating me this way because they are under so much stress... drinking so much ... are unhappy with themselves right now. etc...."*

But all you see is the reflection of your love in their eyes —an illusion. Like a reflection, the emotional depth of a narcissist is only skin deep.

Echo lived on. This experience shattered her. She was just a formless echo blown about by the wind for a while. Then, she established healthier relationships. She became the beloved of Pan, the god of the forests. Mother Gaia took a liking to Echo and spread her voice around the planet to comfort the lonely. The shepherds venerated her and made whistles and instruments to play tunes that Echo could sing back to them. Yes, Echo lives on today.

She survived, and she thrived.

Survival Technique 3

Echo Method

Intense release and reprogramming

This is a form of self-gestalt therapy designed to help you free frustration and emotions that are keeping you stuck and immobilised in this relationship. This therapy resulted from coupling Primal Scream therapy with self-hypnosis. After practising this with clients for 30 years, I can tell you that this simple technique works. So often, people in abusive relationships are like a tightly coiled spring inside a straight jacket. They are very good at suppressing and repressing. This critical technique allows you to unbottle and reconnect. It frees the mind and body to refocus on the future, not just stay stuck in holding it together. It triggers the safety release valve on the emotional pressure cooker. It is safe. This technique may be challenging for some people, but it is essential. Don't skip it. It will help you begin to sing a newer, happier song.

1. In a narcissistic relationship, you will be feeling isolated and lonely. Your partner is not listening to

you. You may feel that no one is listening to you. So you are going to listen to yourself. You will begin to tell yourself the things you need to hear.

2. Choose a time and a space where you can be alone - when your partner is out or at work.

3. Play some music you like (Gloria Gaynor's "I Will Survive" is an excellent standard for this method)

4. Go into a room by yourself. Switch off any phones or screens in the room. No interruptions.

5. Get a large clean bucket or waste paper container and place a large cushion or pillow on the bottom.

6. Select one of the following phrases:
    a. I deserve to be spoken to with respect.
    b. I deserve to be treated with respect.
    c. I deserve to be treated with tenderness.
    d. I deserve healthy love.
    e. I have done nothing wrong (Yes, two negatives can make a positive or, more positively, "I am in the right." Use whichever you feel more comfortable with)

f. (You may write your own unique reprogramming phrase, but it should be couched in the positive)
_____
_____

7. Sit or stand.

8. Hold the bucket up in front of your face. Place your face in the bucket and repeatedly yell the chosen phrase.

   It will muffle the sound effectively yet amplify it back into your ears. It prevents you from having to worry about other people hearing you. Yell it or scream it into the bucket. Let your frustrations out with this. Vent! Repeat for 5+ minutes or until exhausted - Aim for 20 minutes of repetition for maximum effect.

9. Lay on your bed.

10. Acknowledge whatever emotions that wash over you and come to the surface.

Sadness, Tears, Anger or maybe even laughter. Just allow yourself to feel and breathe for another 10 -20 minutes.

11. When the vented emotions run their course through your body, and you feel calm and clear, you may leave the room.

IMPORTANT> Wait to leave the room until you are feeling calm.

Why Echo Fell For a Narcissist

Let's analyse the myth of Echo so that Narcissistic Abuse Victims (NAV) may see their reflection in the first mass media tale of an abusive Narcissist.

Narcissists Don't Fall in Love.

They cannot love another as they are already in love with themselves. The only voice they will hear is their own. Remember, "Love is Listening." So, a narcissist is not interested in listening to another. Therefore, a Narcissist looks for people who will swallow, hook, line and sinker the jazzy lines they throw out about themselves. Once they start hearing their own stories repeated back to them, they know they have added another follower to their throng.

> Echo repeated everything that Narcissist told her. Perfect fit for a Narcissist.

Narcissists Need Helpful People Around Them.

People who can do things for them. Useful people. People who are eager to help are turned towards any task by the manipulative narcissist. They will often target people with status or special skills that can help them with their goals of greater self-aggrandisement. To keep the helpful person with them, they keep the victim locked in a loop. The classic loop is the 'Come here, I need you' and 'Go away, you're not helping' loop. The Narcissist will draw the helper in by telling them they need help and implying that their selected target is the only person who can help them. Then they will do everything to make the person leave, even tell them to leave. Then, when the helper goes to leave, they will imply that the helper never really wanted to help, didn't try hard enough or was too useless. Thus, the helper tries harder and stays in the destructive loop. This is how narcissists get people to act against their self-interest.

> Echo was chronically helpful to anything she thought was hurt. The people most at risk from Narcissism are those helping the strays, the

wounded, the lost, the addicts and the disadvantaged. Echo felt compelled to help; additionally, she was a beautiful, magically divine creature—a perfect fit for a Narcissist.

Narcissists Seek Out Altruistic People.

The more altruistic, the better. All the Narcissist has to do to manipulate the altruist is to make them feel that they are in agreement and that the narcissist may even hold an option that is a cut above that of the targeted altruist. Narcissists find them easy to manipulate. All they have to do is imply that their altruistic targets act hypocritically to their stated ideals. The altruist will try harder to prove they are not hypocritical, whilst the narcissist manipulates the target to point their renewed effort into the narcissist's desired outcome. The narcissist most often targets altruists with status, whilst the commonly placed altruists will be derided for their foolishness. Altruists can find their nobility landing them in life-threatening situations because of the narcissist.

Echo had extreme views about hunters, animals, relationships, how to fairly treat people who have been unfaithful and music. Many of these views were in contrast to or a cut above the generally held opinions of her time. She had lost something very precious to her because of her altruism, which is a big flashing light to the narcissist. If an altruist is willing to give something up for an ideal, they can be manipulated into giving something up for the narcissist. Additionally, Echo had status. Her altruism held her there by his side to be his death companion, even though she could do nothing to help him overcome his deadly vanity. Because of his altruism, she stayed by his side, witnessing the pathetic horror of his death, knowing she was in mortal danger herself, even though she knew this would affect her negatively—a perfect fit for a Narcissist.

Narcissists Look for Victims Who Have Already Been Victims.

There is life after a relationship with a narcissist. However, the victim must consciously choose not to repeat their patterns of abuse. They need to look for the signs and avoid them. Narcissists seek people who have been the victims of an abusive narcissistic relationship before. It's like a moth to a bright light for them. They know that if their victim has done it once before, they can be made to do it again, especially if the target is still living in the victim role. The "poor me" attitude is like a strong pheromone attractant to narcissists. Narcissists are often initially present as a rescuer, saviour, or comforter for the previous abusive relationship. It is so crucial for people who have been in an abusive relationship to spend time alone before they move into another relationship. Former victims of narcissism must have time to themselves to grow strong and educate themselves as to why and how they were manipulated. They need to study their patterns and be aware of their own behaviours in a loving relationship so that they never recreate a similar scenario. The definition of stupidity is doing the same thing over again and expecting a different result. Yet, I see so many women demanding this of the universe. The result is that each successive abusive relationship is worse than the last until, in many cases, they forfeit their own lives. I will never tell you, "What doesn't kill you will make you stronger." I have too many quadriplegic friends in wheelchairs to believe that. However, self-examination will make you wiser and wiser means you will make better choices for your future.

Echo had been the victim of Hera's (represents the mother figure) narcissistic attack. Zeus (represents the father figure) narcissistically lets Echo take the fall for him. The consequences were far more severe for Echo than they would have been for him, but he still threw her under the bus even though she was trying to help him. Artemis (who represents the boss/authority figure) withholds her advocacy and patronage as she morally judges Echo without compassion—a narcissistic trait. Echo had an established pattern of being a Narcissistic Abuse Victim (NAV) pattern —a perfect fit for a Narcissist.

The Narcissistic Parent

In the myth of Echo, we have seen that both of her parental figures behaved in a narcissistic way towards her. This built up her tolerance for being mistreated before she met Narcissus. We have to examine if abuse by our parents has primed us to accept, and indeed seek out as 'normal' for us, an abusive narcissistic relationship later in our adult life.

There are three main kinds of narcissistic parents:

Engulfing Narcissists

These are parents who see their children as extensions of themselves. Engulfing narcissistic parents may become obsessively involved in your life to an extreme extent. They don't respect your boundaries or acknowledge you as a separate person. Former child film and sports stars are one of the most at-risk groups for developing mental health issues such as PTSD. Child Star Syndrome is a term used to describe the troubled adult lives of former child stars. It is a complex and nuanced phenomenon, but key causes include early childhood Engulfing Narcissistic Abuse, emotional, sexual or financial, by parents who famously exploit their work and, in some cases, steal their money.

Using Narcissists

These are parents who have very little interest in their children's welfare. They see the boundary between themselves and their children except where the children can be useful to them. Narcissistic parents can pass parental responsibility onto the child's shoulders so that the child will end up parenting the irresponsible adult. They may treat them like slaves. To cover for this, the user parent may claim the child is lazy and doesn't do enough at home, inducing manipulative guilt in the child whilst gaslighting them to others at the same time. They raise their children to be enablers for a drug habit or attention. This guilt-driven abuse is harrowing to break and can be utilised by the Using Narcissist parent through the child's life to make the adult child feel like they can never do enough for the parent. There is never any gratitude shown to the child, only ever-increasing demands for attention, services, substances and money. Munchausen syndrome, by proxy, is a narcissistic mental disorder that causes a parent or other caretaker to exaggerate, fabricate, or induce illness in a person under their care to obtain financial gain, sympathy or attention. In extreme cases Using narcissistic parents convince the child that they are sick, school them on what to tell the doctors and may even let healthy children undergo dangerous medical treatments in order to sustain an ongoing health benefit payment.

Ignoring Narcissists

These are parents who have very little interest in their children. The Narcissists are only concerned about their own lives. Ignoring narcissists sees the boundary between themselves and their children. But the care factor is zero. They neglect to care for their children or show an active interest in their lives.

Learning to understand and make peace with your childhood abuse is one of the most empowering things you can do. It frees you. The repeating patterns start to unravel and stop repeating. Your subconscious stops seeking a partner that mirrors your narcissistic parent in a vain attempt to recreate and heal the relationships that failed us so painfully in the past. You can see it for what it is and consciously choose not to go there ever again.

As a severely physically, sexually, mentally and emotionally abused adopted daughter of a medicinal drug-addicted mother and absent father, I know how important it is to come to terms with your parents' struggle to live within their narcissistic relationship. Acknowledging that our parents could not have done a better parenting job because of their mental health issues allows us not to be defined by them. The conscious choice about who and what we want to be is based upon acknowledging our experiences, leaving them behind in the past, and moving forward from here.

No matter what happens to us in our childhood, we make our decisions about the person we choose to be. Our childhood does not need to define us; it need not be the excuse we use for our pathologies. A psychologist who listened to my childhood story broke down sobbing and exclaimed, "With everything that has happened to you in childhood, you should have become a serial killer. It is to your credit that you haven't." As disturbing as this was, it made me vividly remember the moment I raised my little clenched fist to the sky and swore to everything divine that I would never be like the people who raised me. Sure, I have made my relationship mistakes, but I have admitted them and gotten out. But I have never set out to victimise anyone. Every day, with every choice we make, we can choose to be a better person. A noble person is not born into royalty. A noble person decides to be their best self.

When we were children, we looked up to our parents for support, encouragement, nurturing and love. But when we were denied these things, we developed a variety of beliefs, behavioural patterns and coping mechanisms to help us survive in such a challenging environment. As adults, we often play out these exact coping mechanisms, often to our detriment.

The thing about being the child of a narcissistic mother and/or father is that it often contributes to something known in shamanic terminology as soul loss. Soul loss is the inability to contact or experience parts of our souls, our core emotional self, due to the unresolved wounds, traumas and fears we've accumulated over the years. Abused children become very good at escaping the harsh reality of their painful lives. They may experience the soul travelling to other realms or alternate realities. To protect themselves, they may leave their tender or spiritual part in these alternate realities where it is safe. Much like a wolf caught in a trap will chew off its foot. This can result in the person appearing to be soulless and uncaring through having trauma-acquired autism. It can make it hard for the person to have regular social interaction, and they can gravitate back to unhealthy social interaction for a sense of familiarity. Monash University has done an exciting study relating the occurrence of people who claim to be psychic or have paranormal experiences having severely abusive childhoods. The correlation is very high. This metal escaping from painful experiences into "another place" appears to be a natural human mechanism, which can make it hard to focus on the experiences of a painful childhood.

You must be willing to explore what you went through as a child to feel comfortable in healthy, loving relationships. This process of exploring the narcissistic actions of your parent isn't done to condemn them or to victimise yourself. Instead, this process is done to help you understand the root cause of any pain you're still experiencing, to learn how to release it, and to move on with your life. This becomes a strengthening and rejuvenating process.

If you're the child of a narcissist, you will likely struggle with these problems:
- Anxiety or depression
- Trust issues
- Being a people pleaser
- Weak sense of self
- Codependency in other relationships
- Inability to express or handle emotions
- Poor interpersonal boundaries
- Inability to say "no"
- Chronic guilt or shame
- Self-loathing
- Emptiness

Survival Technique 4

Identifying The Narcissistic Parent

A narcissistic mother/father will teach you to believe that YOU are the crazy, imbalanced one. That you are the problem in the family, not them. They will gaslight you to other members of the family and won't be happy until they convince everyone that the bad things happening in the family are because of you and not them. This causes you to doubt yourself.

You might suspect something is "off" with your parents as a child. They will make you feel ashamed to think about them in such a way; This can cause you to struggle with guilt.

Did you have a narcissistic mother and/or father?

1. Did your parents ever ask you about your feelings? Yes/No ___
2. Did they display care, empathy or sympathy with you? Or did they seem to be solely interested in their feelings? Yes/No___

3. Did your parent only show you love when you did what they wanted you to do?
Yes/No ___
Example: Parents that used love manipulatively. They withdrew love very easily. If you failed to do what they wanted, they would punish you severely or give you the silent treatment. You thought they only loved you when you PROVED your worth to them.

4. Did your parents try to control you through co-dependency? Yes/No ___
Example. Did your parent/s say, "Don't leave me? I need you. I can't live without you." Making it impossible for you to live an autonomous life or establish independent priorities other than catering to the needs of your parent/s.

5. Were you expected to "parent" your parent? Yes/No ___
Example: Did you become a surrogate parent to cater for their needs instead of them catering to yours?

6. Did your parents lay the guilt on thick? Yes/No ___

Example: Did they constantly guilt trip you into doing what they wanted? They may have told you, "I've done so much for you; I've sacrificed *everything* for you." As a result, you felt indebted to them and as though you "owed" them.

7. You realised that why lied to you all the time? Yes/No ___

Example: Your parent/s lied to manipulate, control and take advantage of you in some way, shape or form. You never knew what you could trust was "real" or truthful around them or whether they were setting up a hidden trap for you to fall into.

8. They never cared about your feelings and desires? Yes/No ___

Example: They never listened when you tried to explain your feelings. You could never share your feelings with your parent/s because they would trivialise you or talk about themselves instead. Your childhood issues were spun into a pity party for them.

9. There was no room for your ideas or desires; they would punish you if you didn't do things their way. Yes/No ___

Example: The message was apparent, "Obey me, or I'll punish you." You were punished through emotional or physical abuse, including emotional blackmail, hitting or beating.

10. Were you constantly insulted by them? Yes/No ___
Example: Your parent/s berated, demeaned and harassed you constantly. They may have even latched onto an insecurity of yours and used it to humiliate you.

11. Your boundaries were never respected? Yes/No ___
Example: Every parent has to check up on their children now and again. However, was there a "private" space to call your own growing up? Did your parent walk into the bathroom while you were using it? Did your parents take things from you with an attitude of if it is yours, it is mine as you owe me everything? Would they use things they knew you wanted to keep private against you?

12. Were they competitive towards you? Yes/No ___

Example: Did they flirt with your dates? Try to make your pet like them better than you. If you got something nice, would they break it or take it from you? If you bought something nice that you were proud of, would they belittle it or buy something nicer to "outdo" you?

13. Did they belittle or distract away from your accomplishments? Yes/No ___

Example: Whenever someone complimented you, your parent/s would instantly jump in and shift the attention to themselves. For instance, if someone congratulated you for winning a sports trophy, your parent/s would butt in and say something along the lines of, "Yes, she gets it from me. I was always athletic as a child." They love the spotlight and frequently steal it from you.

14. Would your parents scream at you and/or physically hurt you if you dared to criticise them? Yes/No ___

Example: Did you ever criticise your mother or father? What was their general reaction? If your mother and/

or father were a narcissist, they likely reacted extremely.

15. Did your parents like to "get even" with you? Yes/No ___

Example: If you did something against their will, they punished you spitefully or in the extreme? Did they behave in a petty and childish way, like the school bully breaking something you cared about deeply or deliberately sabotaging an opportunity to get back at you?

16. Did your parents Gaslight you? Yes/No ___

Example: Did they deliberately make you feel crazy or cause you to doubt your sanity to gain the upper hand? Did you feel constant self-doubt during your childhood and adolescence?

17. Would your parents project their bad behaviour onto you? Yes/No ___

Example: If arguing, would they start screaming at you, " Go to your room. We'll talk after you stop screaming at me." Even though you were not screaming…

18. Were they "Never Wrong"? Yes/No ___

Example: Did they have to be infallible? Did they never apologise for their mistakes? If you confronted them about an error, would they try to spin the blame onto you or others?

19. Was there a "golden" child and a "scapegoat" child in your family? Yes/No ___

Example: Was one child seen as perfect and capable of doing no harm whilst the other child was seen as the black sheep and the cause of all issues

20. Did your parent/s go to great lengths to ensure that others perceived your family as a loving/successful/enviable family?

Example: Were they very concerned about the appearance/status of the family to others?

If you answered yes to any of these questions, please rate them on a scale of 1- 10 regarding how frequently they occur - 1 being hardly ever and 10 being always. If your score is between 20 and 200, you must work to release this early pain. Many narcissist support groups recommend cutting off contact with such parents or interacting with them in small, measured ways.

Note that these score interpretations are self-examinations. They are not a clinical diagnosis.

Healing Your Inner Child

You may feel broken; it's important to remember that you are not broken. Your pain is causing this. But you can release the pain from the past. Your pain will recede, but YOU will still be there. Your authentic self is waiting for you to stop living in the past with things that hurt you then and start living in the now. If others have hurt you in the past, you do not have to let them keep hurting you now. How you choose to live now is your choice. Let go! You can decide to leave the pain of the past behind you. However, letting go is a process. A recovery process.

Ostriches stick their head in the sand but leave most of their body vulnerable. Denial makes you vulnerable. A good recovery process will make you whole and present in the now.

If you had narcissistic parent(s), to make a recovery, you would need to allow yourself to grieve the parent you never had. As with a narcissistic partner, you will also have to stop hoping that your narcissistic parent will change. You have to call a spade a spade and accept them as they are. You can never change them.

A parent is more intrinsic to an individual's sense of self than a partner. We sprang from them. Yet, their bad behaviour does not need to define us. The young of any healthy animal will grow and eventually leave the nest. To have never received the nurturing environment you required in your formative years leaves you craving it. You have to accept that you will never get it from them before you can create a loving and nurturing environment for yourself elsewhere.

You must not continue to allow yourself to be the safe target for their attacks nor the victim of their manipulations. Recovery is impossible under these circumstances. As with a narcissistic partner, if parents behave badly, you need to remove yourself from the situation. Do not be drawn into any further games or manipulations. Don't be drawn back into old patterns with them. Walk away, leave the room or even go out for a while. You may have to block them or change your phone number if you are getting harassed virtually or receiving textual abuse. You may have to change locations. You may have to move far enough away to not be in striking distance. If they are highly abusive, you may have to decide to stay away from them for the sake of your recovery.

Grey Rock

The name "grey rock" refers to becoming as unresponsive as a rock towards people trying to abuse you. Many children who have suffered abuse learn to do this automatically. They become so good at not reacting to people that later in life, they can be diagnosed with acquired autism. Grey Rock technique should always be used cautiously. It is not about learning to endure and abuse. Abuse should never be endured long-term. Long-term use of the grey rock technique can impair your emotionality and social interactions with other people. Grey rock is a technique that is useful for adults in the short term. However, learning to become socially interactive again may be part of the recovery process for people who have had abusive parents.

The Grey Rock technique is used to divert a toxic person's behaviour by acting as unresponsive as possible when you're interacting with them. This method involves:

1. avoiding eye contact,
2. not showing emotions during a conversation,
3. communicating in an uninteresting way when interacting with a narcissist
4. avoiding interactions

I prefer physically removing yourself from their proximity as this is safer, and they cannot abuse you if you are not there.

Silence

Then, be silent. Silence is power. It is the space in which you can recharge and recover. For a while, until you are more robust, don't reach out to them or check in on them. Don't answer your phone or text messages from them, don't interact on social media with them, and you may have to block all digital communications. In extreme cases, you may never be able to see them again. This is never easy, but often it is necessary. You may desperately want their love, but if they are abusive, then they are not acting like a parent, and they don't deserve your love.

Survival Technique 5

Assessing Responsibility to an Abusive Parent

People who argue for their right to remain an abused child of victimising parents by saying, *"...but they will always be my mother/father. I have a responsibility."* In response to them, I often use the example of Diane Downs, the Narcissistic mother who, in Springfield, Oregon, USA, on 19 May 1983 at approximately 10:48 pm, shot her three children because her lover told her he would never marry a woman with children. She manufactured a carjacking story to cover for it. She went to the hospital to try to persuade her surviving daughter to participate in the lie with her. When she wouldn't, Dianne scared her daughter so severely that she had a stroke. It is the chilling tale of a mother's mental illness and unthinking cruelty. The mother has never apologised to her daughter.

1. Do you feel that Diane Down behaved like a mother? Yes/No ___

2. Do you feel that Diane Down has forfeited her motherly rights? Yes/No ___
3. Do you feel that Diane Down's surviving child owes her anything? Yes/No ___
4. Do you think this surviving child should go to visit her mother in jail? Yes/No ___
5. Ask yourself, if you were her daughter, would you ever want to see that woman who tried to kill and then coerce you ever again? Yes/No ___
6. What effect would seeing her mother again have on the surviving child?

_____

_____

_____

_____

7. If you were foster caring for this child, wouldn't you want to protect the daughter from more suffering by seeing her mother again? Yes/No ___
8. Then why would you respect yourself less than the child you were trying to protect?

_____

_____

If you answered yes to any of these questions, please rate them on a scale of 1- 10 regarding how frequently they occur - 1 being hardly ever and 10 being always. If your score is between 20 and 120, you must work to release this early pain. Many narcissist support groups recommend cutting off contact with such parents or interacting with them in small, measured ways.

Note that these score interpretations are self-examinations. They are not a clinical diagnosis.

We all know that parents are responsible for protecting their children, legally and morally. Parents have a responsibility to foster healthy growth in the children they are responsible for. The case with your narcissistic parents may not have been as extreme as Diane Down's, but it can still be toxic and destructive to you. While any person is behaving in a narcissistic or destructive way towards you, it isn't very smart to be around that person.

Earning Forgiveness

Disturbingly, I have read many professionals urging their clients to forgive their parents. This is not healthy and is dangerous to you, as it can prolong abuse. Forgiveness has to be earned. Forgiveness given without being earned will allow you to be open to being hurt again. Forgiveness is not earned by the abuser simply saying: "Oh, I'm sorry." Or worse yet, "Oh, I didn't realise that would hurt you. I only did that because I love you." That is not earning forgiveness. Forgiveness requires a lot more than somebody just asking for forgiveness. An honest and open dialogue, initiated by the parent who is seeking forgiveness and wants to know what they can do to earn forgiveness, is very different from the abusive parent who wants to dismiss or deny responsibility for what they have done. Otherwise, it is a useless gesture. Actions and effort must be put into earning forgiveness over time, proving that forgiveness is indeed warranted.

We colloquially say that 'forgiveness has to be "earned,"' that is because, as a victim, you are paying the price of their abusive actions. On an emotional level, Newtonian physics can apply to the act of forgiveness. Think of it as actions, reactions and cost. Their actions have created this reaction within you. It cost you so much pain, and you have lost so much of your life because of it. Forgiveness will cost them as well. We are not talking about a financial cost here. If they genuinely want forgiveness, it will cost them time, effort and energy. It must be earned. Not expecting forgiveness to be earned shows a lack of respect for the self. However, you can release pain from the past while still expecting your parents in the present and future to earn your forgiveness. If they don't put in this effort, they will never respect you. If they don't put in the effort, then you have to accept the fact that your parent does not want to be forgiven and may simply be trying to manipulate you again and should be treated by you as an ongoing abuser.

Understanding and reframing are different to forgiveness. It can allow you to see the problem from a fresh perspective. Understanding how they were when they were children, you can forgive where they came from and what they endured to end up the way they are. A narcissist is an individual damaged by the abuse they experienced at the hands of a parent or caregiver. A narcissist is re-enacting the horrors, trauma, cruelty and aggression they experienced in their childhood. They choose to repeat the unhealthy patterns of abuse they experienced in childhood. It is a choice to continue that way; they know this behaviour is unacceptable, but they continue to repeat what they grew up with rather than try to learn another way. People are responsible for their adult choices and how they treat others. There are no excuses for bad behaviour. Nor can you excuse bad behaviour in the future or freely forgive what they have not earned the right to have forgiven.

Learn to take care of your own needs through the practice of self-love. Reconnect with your inner child and learn how to care for it in a way your parents never could. It is, however, imperative that you do not let things that have happened in the past continue to hurt you now. You must not live in the past, but you do need resolution. You must release. And you must forgive yourself for allowing yourself to be hurt for so long. To do that, we will take you on an inner journey.

Survival Technique 6

A Journey to Your Inner Child

Performing the following visualisation/guided meditation can help you emotionally reframe the situation with your abusive, narcissistic parents. The more precise that you visualise this, the stronger the result. Take time to allow yourself to feel this. Don't just read through this and forget it. Take time to make this an event for yourself. Please read through it more than once. Then, prepare a space for yourself as follows:

- Get yourself into a warm, comfortable, safe place with dimmed lights. Sometimes, a warm bath is a great place to relax and be guaranteed privacy. However, this can be done anywhere, as long as it is quiet and you won't be interrupted.
- Relax, take ten deep breaths.
- Allow yourself to visualise.
- See yourself as a small child of 10 or younger.
- Feel how you felt when you were a small child.
- Step back from this scene and observe yourself as that small child. Happy, Cute. Carefree.

- Then, the scene darkens, and you see yourself receiving abuse.
- See yourself alone, crying and vulnerable.
- Stay one step removed from this scene. See yourself; you are the observer.
- How do you feel seeing this child receive abuse at the hands of its parents?
- You want to help that child. You want to reach out. It is natural to protect a child. To care for them. To look after them. This child is not being cared for, not properly. It is not being looked after.
- You can reach out to this child. Reach out to the small, frightened, crying child that was you when you were young.
- Let yourself reach out and embrace this child. Give it comfort. Hug this child and tell this child that everything is okay. That it will be okay because you are okay. That in the future, you know that everything will be okay.
- Take this child into your arms. Cradle the child. Comfort the child. Nurture of the child. Rock the child slowly backwards and forwards, allowing the

child to feel the beating of your calm, rhythmic heart.
- The child calms down and becomes content. It feels as though the child is asleep.
- Hug the sleeping child tightly. Know that this child is still sleeping inside of you.
- Consciously feel this child becoming part of you again.
- As you hold the child, you feel the child moving back into your heart.
- Allow the child to become very, very small. Small enough to fit into your heart.
- Find a safe spot inside your heart where you know you can protect the child.
- You love this child. How could you not? Allow the child to feel loved, safe and protected. Allow the child to rest safely in your heart, content and happy.
- Further step back from the scene and see your parents, mother and father.
- See them as they are and as they were then.
- Take a further step back until you can see your parents shrinking to the size of small children. You can see your parents as small children.

- You know they have been abused; you're not sure how, but you know they have.
- They are crying and frightened, unsure of their future.
- Both of them are also in need of comfort.
- Take them in your arms. Give them comfort as you would do for any small child.
- As you do so, you can see the cycle of abuse. It stretches back through generations, from parent to parent. You know that you will break that chain. You know the cycle of abuse ends with you. You consciously choose a different path for your descendants.
- You realise that your parents were victims of victims of victims, acting out as their parents and their parent's parents have done. That does not excuse it. However, no small child should have to go through this. No small child should have to suffer as they have suffered.
- Rock them slowly backwards and forwards, and you feel them shrinking as well, getting smaller and smaller until they are content, quiet, calm, comforted, and small enough to fit inside your heart.

- Place the small children, who were your parents, inside your heart and let them rest peacefully and contentedly for the first time in this incarnation.
- See your child in your heart, greet them, and offer to play with them. See all three children playing contentedly inside your heart.
- See your parents for what they are: small, wounded children.
- It is pointless holding resentment and being angry at small children. Release all of the resentment, all of the anger, all of the pain associated with these wounded children.
- Allow the children to live in peace inside your heart where they can play together.
- Return your consciousness to yourself as an adult. Feel lighter. You are feeling freer and know that you do not have a desire to fix things any more with your parents. Knowing that you can release them and see that you will no longer allow yourself to be disrespected by any bad behaviour from these childish people.
- Do not demand anything from them emotionally. Not expecting anything. No expectations. Simply

release. Let go and know that you will never allow them to injure that small child in your heart again.
- If they do not treat you with respect, you will step back. You will see them as small, injured children, but you will not participate in any spiteful games.
- You will protect your inner child, keeping it warm and safe and loved and nurtured, and you will be free.

This experience only serves to show you that everything you need is within you. No matter your childhood, it's still possible to heal and reunite with that source of unconditional love, wonder and joy.

Survival Technique 7

Narcissism Self-Check

Children of narcissistic abuse are vulnerable to becoming either victims of other narcissists or narcissists themselves. Contrary to popular belief, the majority of narcissists are not evil geniuses. They are repeating a dysfunctional pattern they have acquired from dysfunctional parents. That leaves them with a deeply entrenched sense of grief. Via this grief, they can also hook into a victim's grief. Thus, the cycle begins to repeat for both the potential abuses and the potential victims. Many people do not want to acknowledge that narcissists have been victims themselves. Much of their manipulation of others occurs on a subconscious level as they try to force their victims into the parenting role of accepting all responsibility for their actions. Because they did not receive correct emotional care from their parent when they were young, they have not learnt to be able to value, share or express emotions. Therefore, the desire to be the centre of parental attention begins by making the victim the centre of their attention, giving them the love they missed out on giving to a parent.

At the start of a narcissistic relationship, many victims report feeling overwhelming love and attention from the narcissist. The narcissist will often go out of their way initially to make the victim feel like the centre of the world. By making them feel like the centre of the world, the narcissist focuses the attention on the victim, thereby making the victim feel guilty that they may be a narcissist. This opens the gate for effective gaslighting.

All people display some narcissistic traits. However, as children of narcissists, we have to be aware that we may have learned some of their bad habits. Professor Samuel Vaknin suggests in several of his works that victims of narcissistic abuse have to be on guard against being forced into narcissistic behaviours themselves.

A process of self-examination will allow us to check and ensure that we are not actively participating in any inherited disorders. We are all on the narcissistic spectrum somewhere. It is healthy to be concerned about yourself. There are times in our lives when more self-concern is needed for showmanship, creativity or even self-preservation. However, when this self-concern becomes an obsession or a disorder, that's when there are problems. This quick quiz will help you determine where you are on the spectrum:

1. Do people tell you that you take up all the space in the room? Yes/ No____
2. Do conversations with you so frequently take an "it's all about me" turn? Yes/ No____

3. When others express their feelings and concerns, is your reaction "Well, what about me?" Yes/ No___
4. Do you find that instead of valuing others' inputs and sharing equal air time, discussions become monologues where you pontificate, assuming you know best? Yes/ No___

How well a person listens to others is a primary indicator of narcissism.

Healthy people in healthy relationships can listen responsively to their concerns and others. They can be self-centred in the best sense (taking care of themselves) and altruistic (taking heed of others' desires). Excessive altruism invites co-dependency and enabling behaviours.

5. Do you desire to understand what's interesting in what others say? Yes/No___
6. Do You disparage or ignore others' input? Yes/ No___
7. Are you all about others? Yes/No___

Bilateral Listening

The ability to hear oneself and others is bilateral (2-sided) listening. The ability to do bilateral listening enables the creation of win-win solutions. This creates sustaining ongoing goodwill in relationships. When differences arise, can you consider both your concerns and others?

8. Do you compromise if you are watching TV with your partner/friend - to find a program that you will both enjoy? Yes/No___ or
9. Do you always end up watching what you want? Yes/No___

If you are tired and have just received a call from a friend who has a problem and urgently wants to talk, do you...

11. Suggest that the two of you talk at least for a few minutes now and plan to talk more at length in the morning. Yes/No___ or
12. Respond with an immediate" *No. I'm too tired.*" Yes/No___

Generosity

Often, narcissistic individuals can show compassionate generosity toward strangers yet not to the people they are supposed to love. They may be very charitable in public to try to display compassion and altruism. Family members may be treated meanly, while those with power or wealth get treated with generosity. If a narcissist wants something, the possibility that it is in conflict with what someone else wants is not a consideration?

13. Do you run over others to get what you want? Yes/No___

14. If you are out with a friend for lunch at a bakery and your friend tells you how good the mille-feuilles are at this bakery and how much they love them. When it is your turn to order, there are only two left. Do you order both for yourself, because if they are that good, you will want another? Yes/No___ or

15. If there is only one left, do you order it and give it to your friend, and have something else yourself? Yes/No___

If you scored 1 to 20, you have ordinary healthy self-interest. If you feel guilty for answering positively to any of these questions, then you need to be careful not to put others' interests ahead of yours too often. If you scored 20 to 50, then there are some unhealthy narcissistic tendencies there, and you are aware of them. We all have moments where we are less tolerant of others and more interested in ourselves. It can vary from day to day. It's when they become consistent habits that they become a problem. If you score 50 to 150, then you have acquired some narcissistic habits that you need to address.

This quiz is not intended to diagnose any narcissistic personality disorders. It is designed to heighten self-awareness and does not replace working with a qualified therapist.

Narcissistic disorders are a people skills deficit. Victim-acquired narcissistic traits and acquired patterns of behaviour may cause some conflict in reading this book on recovery from narcissistic abuse and being asked what narcissistic characteristics you feel you exhibit. We're not talking about intermittent behaviours. Intermittently, everyone behaves increasingly narcissistic when angry. Angry people want to be right. Anger blocks your ability to see another's point of view and intensifies your focus on yourself and your issues. It stops you from listening to other people. We will all get angry at different times; that is part of the human condition. Yet, if these narcissistic patterns become habitual, awareness allows us to correct them before they become ingrained.

If you are uncomfortable with your score, remember that mild "narcissism" is a habit pattern, and habits can be changed. It is human nature to acquire good and bad habits from the people around us. Unfortunately, it is far easier to acquire bad habits than the good ones. The theory of Stockholm Syndrome shows that victims start to identify with abusers. However, you can only produce changes in yourself with awareness. Suppose you have acquired some of these habits. In that case, they can be rectified by consciously choosing to remain calm in conflict situations and upgrading your listening and shared decision-making skills. Stepping out of these habits is part of stepping out of victim consciousness and re-taking control of your life.

Narcissistic Religions and Cults

A "cult" is a group or movement that is held together by a common devotion to a charismatic leader or doctrine, according to Merriam-Webster. It has a belief system with the answers to all of life's questions and only the leader's laws can provide you with a unique solution.

Throughout human history, there have been people who have presented themselves above others. Be them the white supremacists of the early 20th century, the Nazis of Germany in the 1930s and 40s, or ISIS in more recent years. All of these groups have been deemed cults due to their fanatical following and willingness to commit atrocities in the name of their leader.

Narcissistic abuse does not always come from individuals. Sometimes an abusing narcissist is an organisation or group. An organisation or a group displaying narcissistic traits is called a cult. People who have been abused by individual narcissists are very vulnerable to being absorbed into a narcissistic cult.

Conversely, a person escaping a narcissistic cult must be on their guard to avoid individual narcissists. It is important that people who have suffered narcissistic abuse at the hands of an individual also be able to identify a narcissistic group, to avoid further abuse. It can be harder to escape a narcissistic group than to escape an individual narcissist. However, the principles of escape and recovery from a cult or an individual narcissist are the same. It is also useful to see how many identifying marks cults and individual narcissists share. Becoming aware of the narcissistic nature of cults will also make a person aware of the danger inherent in allowing oneself to remain a long-term victim of a narcissistic individual.

Cults are person-centred organisations where the cult leader is usually infallible or omniscient and above questioning. Cult leaders can be male or female. However, some cults hold "the organisation" itself to be the infallible object on which all must base themselves. Cult leaders dehumanise and objectify people. The family of a narcissist may be run like a cult, with the narcissist as the unquestioned guru whose every wish is obeyed. It usually begins with social interaction with a person who is suffering from some emotional pain. The cult leader offers himself up as the answer to this person's problem. He will claim to have all of the answers and that only he knows the "true way". Sooner than later, the messiah-like figure will start to demand more and more from his followers.

The behaviour of the cult/organisation/leader is textbook narcissism. You may find yourself being the effects of narcissistic abuse. As such, you may find our companion report **"Triumph and Thrive After Narcissistic Abuse,"** useful.

The Author's Story

When I was 10 years of age, my parents converted to becoming Jehovah's Witnesses. The Jehovah's Witnesses argue that their "religion" is not a cult, yet it ticks all of the boxes in the cult checklist. (see the end of this document.) Any attention to the self was discouraged. My natural talent and academic ability were dissuaded. I was offered a modelling and a singing career. The Jehovah's Witness "Elders" of my congregation told me if I pursued these, I would be excommunicated. Their terminology for excommunication is "Disfellowshipping." "Disfellowshipping" is where nobody in "The Organisation" will have anything to do with you. They will not speak to you, give you work or any assistance. If the organisation says you are disfellowshipped, individuals are not allowed to make a personal judgement on how they will treat that person.

Even though, I excelled in their "Theocratic Ministry School," and I was held up as the ideal little Christian girl at their assemblies in front of thousands of people, my father was told not to send me to university as it was useless because Armageddon was coming. I also found myself the victim of an exorcism during my early teen years, as I was deeply, empathetic and intuitive. I had hurt nobody, but I can tell you, that the experience of an exorcism was terrifying and life-threatening. It was considered traitorous to go to the police if there were problems within the organisation. Nothing was ever to be done to embarrass "The Organisation." The elders handled all illegal matters internally. Including many the many incidences of child abuse that I was aware of, including myself, and my firstborn, son.

An example of this, as I was growing up was the abuse I suffered at the hands of my mother. My adoptive mother was a narcissist and a medicinal drug addict. She abused me physically, emotionally, mentally and sexually until I moved out of the house at seventeen. I still find it difficult to talk about some of the depraved things that she did to me as a child. Her overt abusive behaviour, even in the church meetings, was obvious to The Elders. We were often bashed and swung around by the hair in the meetings. Additionally, she would bring a hat pin – a very large hat pin, into the meetings and stick it into us if we went if we nodded off during the boring bits. The elders would laugh with her about this and quote Proverbs 23:13-14: *"Do not withhold discipline from a child; if you strike him with a rod, he will not die. If you strike him with the rod, you will save his soul from Sheol."*
English Standard Version 2016 (ESV)

When I complained about the sexual abuse and severe beatings, they told me that the Bible said that it was up to a parent to discipline a child however, they see fit. And as a good Christian, I should suffer in silence. "The Elders" just covered up the scandal and tried to handle it internally, rather than go to the police, as they had done with many other cases, that I have become aware of. They were criminally culpable. They knew about the crime and they refused to take it to the police where it should've been taken. That made them just as guilty as the perpetrator. Culpability means that, by their inaction, they're helping the perpetrator.

I was forced into a marriage with an abusive and narcissistic man within the Jehovah's Witnesses. When I went to the elders to ask for their assistance with his abuse, and his repeated infidelity, they told me that a wife should stay with her husband, no matter what, and if I persisted, they would punish me. I screamed and cried and said how unfair and hypocritical it was, and that they should help me so they "disassociated" me. This is a term within the Jehovah's Witnesses for when they will refuse to speak, or have anything socially to do with certain marked members for disciplinary reasons.

Eventually, after much physical violence by my husband, I could stand it no longer, and I left. When I decided to divorce my husband, I was "disfellowshipped". This is what their "organisation" does when they feel people are "worldly" and "unrepentant." This was terrifying as, after 18 years within the organisation, and growing up within its confines, I did not know where to turn and had no contact outside of the cult.

Narcissistic cults often manipulate circumstances where, even powerful people, no longer have income or anywhere to go. Once they are completely dependent upon them and they feel their adherents can't leave, then the abuse starts in earnest. However, these days there are many organisations set up to help recently separated parties and their children fleeing from abuse. A good first stop, and one that I can personally recommend, is the Salvation Army. When I left, The Jehovah's Witnesses, and the father of my second child, I retired to my hometown with nothing. In secret, and without the knowledge of the Jehovah's Witnesses, my father, found me a small cheap flat with a wonderful South American landlord. Mr Pasquale lived on-site and always kept a protective eye on me and my two boys. I felt safe. However, because my father was still a member of the

Jehovah's Witnesses, he was ordered to not have anything to do with his "worldly daughter."

The organisation, I was raised in, follows a narcissistic abuse pattern which was ingrained into me as normal behaviour. It haunted me for the early part of my adult life. Repeating a pattern of narcissism in three relationships. Two personal and one working. However, from day one, the Salvation Army showed my children and me, extreme compassion, with regular food parcels, beds for us to sleep on and a huge bundle of toys for my children, as it was Christmas time. One of the brand-new stuffed toys was bigger than me. My youngest son's eyes got so big in his little face when he saw it, I cried with joy. To me, the six-foot-tall white dog with an elongated neck and short legs was a universal sign. The moment it came to the door, on the 2nd day of our new independent existence, I knew I would have a job soon and that we would be OK. The Salvo's were amazing and, in gratitude, I still donate to them today. They have helped many victims begin to rebuild their lives. Don't be too proud to ask for and receive help with necessities if you need it.

After having been raised by narcissistic parents, in a narcissistic cult religion, that forced me to marry a narcissistic man, I should have been more careful. Yet, after leaving my husband and my religion, I began working for a narcissistic boss who eventually set up a cult for herself! Pattern repeated. People who escape a cult must be very careful, not to settle into a familiar feeling situation.

Ways to prevent the pattern, from repeating, you must remember two things:

1) **Don't Forgive Too Easily.** Let people earn your forgiveness before you begin to trust them again. If you do not do this, they will hurt you again. That means we want to see them put in a serious effort to earn your forgiveness, over some time. Anybody can say anything quickly in the spur of the moment, but actions speak louder than words. Manipulators know how to say exactly the correct emotional thing that will elicit a response from you. When somebody says something, incredibly emotional to you, just say to yourself "Well, we'll see." and take a step back from that person and wait to see if they earn your

forgiveness over a period of time. Forgive only after they have worked hard to earn your forgiveness.

2) **Don't Trust Too Easily.** Trust must be earned. It is a privilege, not a right. Do not begin any relationship based on unearned trust. Remember that there is a danger of you repeating your pattern. So, do not give people the benefit of the doubt, and do not draw them in towards you too quickly. With people recovering from narcissistic abuse, there is a real need for connection. But establishing a real connection with you is a privilege that people need to earn. In Asian culture, it is normal to let people earn your trust before you befriend them, and they think we can. Westerners are crazy for trusting people first and then crying when they get hurt. The people that you draw into your life will affect not only you but also the people around you. You are it to everybody around you to take your time and trust only when trust has been earned.

Though it is vitally important to tell your story, pick only a person who has earned your trust to tell your story too.

You certainly don't want others to view you as a victim or as their potential victim.

I did not tell people about my abuse. It wasn't like my new boss picked me because she knew that I had been abused. She chose me as the right person for the right job at exactly the right moment when she needed someone to fill that position. And I was exactly the right person at exactly the right time. She had an Australian network that taught hospitality to restaurant staff. I became a first-class trainer in silver service and cocktail and bar work. The wages were good. I got to travel around a lot, and I felt empowered. Had no intention of ever telling my boss about the abuse that I had escaped from. A mutual acquaintance, the former boss of my ex-husband, had run through some of the details with her. My boss, as a narcissistic abuser, must have identified me as a potential victim at that point. Even though I did not feel like a victim any more. My boss pretended to befriend me and was very interested in the abuse that I had escaped. She could see that I remained a deeply spiritual person, and she took a great interest in the things I was writing as part of my recovery. She even stole the workbooks and cassette tapes that I was dictating experiences onto when she visited my house. These were the methods that I utilised to recover and strengthen myself. Started to feel suspicious when she kept grilling me about the techniques that the Jehovah's Witnesses used to bastardise people into submission.

One day out of the blue, she told me that she had been putting some workshops together herself and she ordered me to attend several of these courses for $1000 each. I attended one, and to my horror, the workbooks, and the meditations that she distributed were almost word for word from my notes. (Theft and plagiarism) At this course, she insisted that I do the next step. When I refused to become part of the cult, I was sacked. She went on to recruit, vulnerable workshop attendees to come and live in a commune, where she was the undisputed Messiah figure. Many people reported the abuse that they received within this cult. It was extreme abuse and was eventually closed down by the government. The scary thing is that she went on to retrain as a psychologist after her cult was dismantled. She is still practising as a psychologist to this day. To me, that is like putting a child molester to work in child welfare. Which is exactly what happened with my ex-husband. It took me a year to find and rescue my eldest son after his father kidnapped him. In revenge for me, taking my son and becoming successful, my ex-husband created a situation for his son, to be sexually abused. He was shielded by the Jehovah's Witnesses (criminal culpability) but he and the other guilty ones were eventually arrested and charged. He later moved to Perth where he got a job working in child corrections as, in Australia, the child sex offender registry is only effective state by state.

3) **Don't Focus on Justice.** The statements probably shock you. But having dealt with many severely abused women at my centre over decades, I can tell you that justice is a rare thing. Focusing on justice instead of your recovery only prevents your healing. If justice happens, it is a bonus. What you need to do is stop focusing on 'them.' On the perpetrators. On the people outside of you who hurt you. On the organisations set up to hurt people. You need to focus on yourself. On healing, recovering, and becoming powerful. Success always follows after you become

fully empowered again. And always remember that **Success Is the Best Revenge**. The organisations and people that hurt, you will feel that they have fiery coals heaped on their forehead if you are successful. Seeing you burn brightly will burn those who tried to destroy you. Yes. success is the best revenge, and you will be powerful, healed and successful.

As a survivor of narcissistic abuse, you can't focus on revenge or justice you have to focus on your recovery. That is the most important thing. For me, the most important thing was my son's recovery. So I just focused on my son's recovery and retreated to 168 acres of solitude in the bush. I sent my son to a very small country school where they were dedicated to his recovery as well. My life began to prosper. I was awarded Queensland Businesswoman of the Year. I completed psychological counselling studies. I opened my own centre/retreat and finally entered into a relationship with a very, tender, caring, partner named Rick. I was really happy. I had worked through my victim stuff for 10 years. I even ran meet-up groups and workshops for people who were victims of narcissistic abuse. I was nominated for Australian of the Year. Then, after Rick and I amicably separated, I repeated my pattern, and then I had one more hugely narcissistic relationship.

Never let your guard down. Don't break your principles of not trusting until somebody has earned your trust. Remember that your pattern can repeat and always be cautious. I was incautious. All this time I let my guard down. We had been in a long-distance relationship for two years. Even though there were some problems, when he asked me to move in with him, I did. He struck at the right moment. The lease has expired on my rule centre, and he cried, begging that he believed it was time for us to move in together. I stayed with him for only eight weeks in Sydney. Once I moved in, he went through a process of using up my finances by renovating his house and attempting to isolate me. It's started to get very crazy and manipulative. I started to put plans in place in case I needed to move out. Then he hit me and hospitalised me. I moved out the next day. He was so shocked that I could move out so quickly. He thought he had disempowered me in only two months. Wrong! Let me tell you, there are always options and there are always people to help. The people in Sydney, who were around us could see how aggressive he had become, and how bad his manipulations were. They were happy to help me get free. In retaliation, he spread lies and rumours about me back in my hometown in Queensland, thousands of miles away. He was good at the lies. Remember, I had been Queensland Business Woman of the Year, I'd been nominated for Australian of the Year I had run I sent to helping other people for decades. Still, it took years for people in Queensland to realise they had been lied to by him. Then I landed a top-rated TV show. Success again, and he and his lies were forgotten. When he was investigated for the attack on me, they found that he had been using his job at the airport to import steroids illegally, so he fled to the United States. There he began to find new victims in his new country. Jo-Ann, his American wife of 10 years, tells her story in the companion report to this.

I finally broke the cycle and have been in a loving relationship last 24 years.

I don't like talking about my horror stories. But sharing your story is part of recovery. Most importantly, I'm telling the stories because I want you to know that no matter how bad your abuse is, how ingrained the pattern has become. You can break the pattern. You can have a wonderful loving life, where you learn to trust again. And you can thrive. You will be able to use the experiences that you have been through to work towards success. You will find more about that in "Jo's Story" later in this book

For now, let's take you through the eight steps to identify and get yourself free of the abuse from Cults.

1) The Cult's Charismatic Founder or Chieftains are Narcissists

The narcissist claims to be better than others, all others. Likewise, the cult leader's common appellations are: holy, highness, infallible, superior, talented, skilful, omnipotent, and omniscient. The cult must keep its God-like status and omnipotence to continue controlling its victims.

In Nazi Germany, the people were told that the Aryan Race was the master race, destined to rule the world. To achieve this, they needed to get rid of all of the "undesirables" such as Jews, Romani people, homosexuals, and the physically and mentally disabled. The cult leader, Adolf Hitler, convinced his followers that this was the only way to achieve a better future.

A cult leader lies to support these unfounded claims. He expects awe, admiration, adulation, and constant attention commensurate with these outlandish assertions. He reinterprets reality to fit his fantasies and expects all his followers to support and expound these fantasies about him.

Cult leaders are narcissists who withdraw into a "Pathological Narcissistic Space" (PNS): an imaginary environment, a comfort zone, which has clear geographical and physical boundaries. If he fails in one Pathological Narcissistic Space, he relocates and conjures up another as did Rev. Jones. He took his Peoples Temple to Jonestown, Guyana after he was embroiled in scandal and lawsuits in the United States. This was such a pathological narcissistic space it was named after him and based completely on his irrational, changeable ideals. With disastrous results.

2) Cults Are Very Loving at First

Initially, cults, like a narcissistic relationship, are very attentive to you. They feel like a calm safe place where you are assured of the master's unconditional acceptance and love. They claim to be everything you need and will find solutions to any problems you may be facing. They encourage you to be vulnerable, open up and share personal information, but this will be used against you later to exert control if you try and break away from the cult in the future.

For ordinary people, it becomes their second home, and for some, it is the only family they have ever known. A reprieve from a life of insecurity, anxiety, and self-doubt. A chance to be part of something larger than themselves and to feel

3) Cults Practice Brainwashing

New members of cults are broken in by brainwashing and prolonged twisted logic. Twisted logic is where something is reasoned away to defy the known laws of physics. For instance, I can look at the map of the world. The world map is flat, therefore the world must be flat. This is twisted logic. Cults use verbal gymnastics to make their members believe in the most absurd things by breaking down their capacity to reason. This process is called "milieu control" and it's what allows the cult leader to get away with anything.

This doesn't happen overnight, it's a gradual process that happens over time as the new member slowly starts to disconnect from their old life, friends, and family. They become more and more reliant on the cult for their emotional needs to be met.

Long periods of indoctrination, training, and isolationist retreats, are urged, where psychological reconditioning takes place. A new alternative reality is asserted. *"It is real because we all believe it."* They strip you of your individuality, your mindset, and beliefs, *"for the benefit of the group."* You are expected to adopt a group mindset, a forced reality. An 'us against them' mentality is fostered to keep you in the cult.

They will tell the new members they are crazy if they do not believe what they have all awoken to. This is group gaslighting. It creates a mental enclave of suspended judgment which quickly becomes the disciple's comfort zone, devoid of all responsibilities. It is a natural human craving for belonging, to be like your friends. This creates an inclusionary shared psychosis usually focused on proselytisation.

Proselytisation is the recruitment of new members. The more people that can be brought in, the more validation for the cult's shared delusional beliefs. This is how a small group can grow to have a large following and become very dangerous.

Cults attempt to spread the narcissist's message and seek new converts among friends, colleagues, co-workers, fans, churchgoers, and anyone else. Eventually, the cult members become co-dependent enablers of the narcissistic leader and will attack anything that threatens to free them from his control. Group members will police each other when it comes to maintaining expected behaviours and beliefs. They will be intolerant of people who do not hold to the same beliefs as them. Shared psychoses are also common in other settings like business, political activism, ideological movements, and academia.

As a result, hate crime becomes normalised. The leader is above the law and any actions they take are justified in the name of the cause or religion. This is what happened with Jim Jones and the Jonestown massacre. It is also happening now with ISIS.

4) Cults Isolate the Individual

Cults impose an exclusionary shared psychosis. This involves the physical and emotional isolation of the narcissist and his "flock" (spouse, children, fans, friends) from the outside world to shield them from threats and hostile intentions of some all-pervading malevolence.

Cult-based exclusionary or inclusionary shared psychosis, includes persecutory delusions, enemies, mythically grandiose narratives, and apocalyptic scenarios. For instance, the narcissist may believe that he is the reincarnation of Jesus Christ or that he is about to save the world from destruction. The narcissist's family and friends are expected to share these grandiose delusions and to serve as willing accomplices in his nefarious plans.

Cults and their leaders, act in a critical, patronising, and condescending manner, that devalues the cult members. Any individual talents or gifts are minimised. They legitimise subsequent abuse as being for the member's benefit. The cult leader acts in the same isolating way that a private narcissist does with his spouse, his offspring, and other family members.

5) Cults and Narcissists Do Not Respect Personal Boundaries

Cults do not respect the personal boundaries and privacy of adherents. Like a narcissist, they will ignore individuals' wishes and treat them as objects or instruments of gratification. A critical red flag is shunning individuality. It is human nature to want to be included, to want to be like our friends. However, cults, insist on you becoming like them, thinking like them, and viewing the world the way they want you to.

Your feelings, needs, and privacy do not matter. If you do not learn to think exactly like them or at least claim to, you will be ghosted, shunned, disfellowshipped, and ostracised. This is terrifying after the cult's isolation tactics leave the individual feeling they have nowhere to go if they are rejected, cults constantly question new adherents on what they are thinking, what they are doing, and who they are doing it with. Adherents cannot keep anything away from the cult because they are entitled to know everything.

6) Cults Seek to Control Situations and People

As with narcissistic relationships, coercive control pervades all cults. Their manipulative techniques are designed to ensure a victim knows the narcissist/cult is in control. They thrive on making adherents believe that they are superior to the victims. Cults will make rulings that govern every aspect of an adherent's life.

They often downplay these coercive rulings by referring to biblical or divine authority or with statements like: *"Oh! It's just It has been this way for years."* Cult members are expected to 'suffer in silence' through the intrusive attack on their personal lives.

Though they claim to be 'doing this out of love for you, narcissistic cults display zero empathy for an individual's feelings and well-being. The more involved the adherent becomes in the cult the more they are expected to be available to the cult.

Adherents must do what the cult says, as they now belong to them. What's yours is theirs, and everything good that happens for or to you results from their making. These coercive rulings include strong disapproval of personal autonomy and independence. Activities, such as meeting a friend or visiting one's family may require permission. Any such isolationist tactics are red flags.

The cult leader gains leverage and creates uncertainty. The cult thrives on moral conflict. The victim becomes riddled with confusion. Denials create anxiety in a victim, They doubt everything and feel they have done something wrong. All members suffer from enforced adherence to the cult's teachings, and goals. The cult leader feels they are above the law. They never accept blame or criticism and never apologise. They will repeatedly lie and falsify information to avoid accountability. Cults as with all narcissists thrive on an overdeveloped sense of entitlement.

The cult leader will encourage adherents to be hostile to any who seek to oppose or expose him. This will include critics, media, authorities, and institutions, which he will rebrand as his enemies, For this reason, cults usually impose heavy media censorship rules upon their members. Cults will be fed only information that appears to uphold the cult/narcissist viewpoint.

7) Cults Seek to Make You Fully Dependant Upon Them

Cult leaders are great illusionists who use manipulation to make adherents believe they need them. They will charm then harm. Cult members participate in mutual policing, meddling, and reporting on each other's intimate thoughts and moments. This robs victims of their humanity. Gossiping and members backstabbing each other within the cult are encouraged privately, whilst publicly they have big smiles, profess kindness, endorse public charitable gestures, and hold carefully staged photo ops, to hide this base manipulation.

Once you belong to the cult, they will use you as they please whilst gaslighting your reality. They strive to make the adherents fully dependent emotionally, sexually, financially, and socially. Though cults/ narcissists are very loving at the start, as former members try to walk away, the cult seeks to cut them off at their knees, immobilising them with fear. If adherents try to break away they will suffer the consequences, which may include being told terrifying fictional scenarios of divine retribution, shunning, ghosting, loss of support, financial penalties, and sometimes beatings and death threats. Cults work on the fear that when individual freedom, rights, and boundaries have all been stripped away, adherents will have nowhere to go. Always remember that this is a fallacy. Whether you are suffering abuse from a cult or an individual narcissist, there are always people who will help you.

8) Cults Punish Non-Compliance

The narcissist at the centre of a cult, demands complete obedience from his followers. The cult and its leader will try to crush the non-compliant. This is done to protect the image of the cult. The cult leader will have the non-compliant in their sights. They will be waiting for the perfect opportunity to crush the non-compliant and bring them back under their spell. Their dialogue will run the same path as interpersonal conversations with a narcissist.

A cult leader/narcissist will not tolerate any questioning or criticism of himself. He will take criticism of the cult as criticism of himself. Blurring the lines between the two. He will become over-defensive of an innocuous and inoffensive question. He will try to hammer down the nail that has its head sticking up. The cult leader/narcissist's defensive dialogue will run this way:

- Don't challenge me. I always win.
- Don't you know who I am?
- How dare you accuse me?
- I deny all of your accusations.
- People will believe me, not you.

- I defeat any attacks against me.
- Don't you know that you are in the presence of a divine being and you are inconsequential?"

Thought-Terminating Cult Clichés

Cults/Narcissists use similar rhetoric. These short automatic responses are programmed into cult members as answers when they are asked difficult questions:

- *"Now you're one of us, you're part of the family."*
- *"Family/Church is the most important thing."*
- *"We must stay close as a family/brethren."*
- *"We have to stick together, like a family sticks together, no matter what."*
- *"We are all you have"*
- *This is THE (only) Truth/Way/Light of the World."*
- *"Lies of the devil."* is a response to any fact that contradicts any pre-programmed belief.
- *"Let's pray over it."* when something can't be explained away or morally excused.
- *"Everything can be solved with prayer."*
- *"Stop thinking so much."* redirects attention from issues to the abuse of thought itself.

- *"What would Guru/Jesus/Mohamed/God/Leader think about the way you're behaving?"*
- *"Don't mind (the Narcissistic cult leader), they don't mean it that way."*
- *"That's just how they are"*
- *"The congregational elders can solve this situation. You should reach out to them"*
- *"Fake news." is used to negate the source of any fact.*
- *"Don't speak about what goes on within this group to outsiders"*

This programmed rhetoric is used to stop dissent and excuse the abuse within the cult. Members will take great pleasure in reminding you of these mottoes. It makes them feel like authorities. This is done to shut you down as fast as possible. If you hear these phrases, or phrases similar to these, repeated regularly, this should be taken as a huge red signal for you to get away from the group/relationship.

Infamous Cults From The Past and Present

Over the past few centuries, we have seen cults come and go. Some have been relatively harmless, while others have been deadly. Here is a list of some of the most famous cults and their leaders.

The Manson Family

The Manson Family was a cult led by Charles Manson in the late 1960s. The group was based in California and consisted of young, mostly female followers who were drawn to Manson's charisma and ideology. The Manson Family believed that an apocalyptic race war was coming, and they would be able to survive it by hiding out in a secret location known as the "Bottomless Pit." The group's most famous victim was actress Sharon Tate. Manson and several members of his cult were arrested and convicted of murder. Manson is currently serving a life sentence in prison.

The Peoples Temple

The Peoples Temple was a cult led by Jim Jones. The group was based in San Francisco but also had a settlement in Jonestown, Guyana. The cult was responsible for the murders of several people, including US Congressman Leo Ryan. The group's ideology was based on Jones' belief that he was a prophet who had been chosen by God to lead his people to safety. This cult ended with the mass suicide of the Jones Town inhabitants, via self-administration of poison. Horrifically they also poisoned all their little children.

The Aum Shinrikyo

The Aum Shinrikyo is a Japanese cult that was responsible for the 1995 sarin gas attack on the Tokyo subway system. The cult was led by Shoko Asahara, a former star student of the Dali Lama, who preached a mix of Buddhist teachings, with apocalyptic messages. The group was known for its belief in doomsday, and its members were expected to be ready to die at any time. The Aum Shinrikyo was also known for its use of violence and was implicated in several murders and terrorist attacks in the years leading up to the Tokyo attack.

The sarin gas attack was carried out by a group of Aum Shinrikyo members who boarded five separate trains during morning rush hour and released the nerve agent into the cars. Twelve people were killed and over five thousand were injured in the attack, making it one of the deadliest terrorist incidents in Japanese history. The Aum Shinrikyo cult was subsequently banned and its leaders were arrested and imprisoned.

The Branch Davidians

The Branch Davidians is a religious sect that was founded in the 1930s by Victor Houteff. The group is based on the teachings of the Bible and believes in an impending apocalypse. They also believe that their leader, David Koresh, was a modern-day prophet who has been chosen by God to lead them through the end times.

The Branch Davidians gained notoriety in 1993 when they were involved in a standoff with law enforcement at their compound in Waco, Texas. The standoff began after agents from the Bureau of Alcohol, Tobacco, and Firearms raided the compound in an attempt to arrest Koresh. The raid led to a gun battle in which several people were killed, including four ATF agents and six Branch Davidians.

Though this group was a true cult, fitting all the criteria of a cult run by a narcissist, they were not feared to be terrorists. Coroner's inquests and investigations into this calamity have shown the escalation of the stand-off is held to be the responsibility of the bureaucratic system, rather than a result of cult practices. The stand-off could've ended without any casualties if it had been handled differently. This very public tragedy has resulted in the FBI revising the way it is to handle interactions with a nonviolent cult. Cults/narcissists will not bow to the pressure of an outside authority. Head-on conflict with a previously non-violent cult/narcissist can escalate them into violence. It is better to convince them it is their idea to change their stand rather than trying to force them to stand down. The incorrect handling of a narcissist by the authorities has resulted in many tragic hostage situations. These situations can be prevented by utilising a psychologist skilled in negotiating resolutions with a narcissistic personality disorder. It is interesting to note that Koresh requested a negotiator several times during this standoff. Instead, the local authorities tried to intimidate the cult to back down via the use of force. This played into the cult's martyrdom ideology. The standoff ended after 51 days when the FBI launched an assault on the compound. The fire that resulted from the assault killed 76 people, including Koresh.

Klu Klux Klan

Founded in 1865, the Klu Klux Klan is one of America's oldest and most notorious hate groups. The KKK has a long history of violence and terrorism against African Americans, Jews, Catholics, and other minorities. Over the years, the Klan has undergone several changes, but it remains a powerful force in American society.

The Klan was founded by Confederate veterans who wanted to maintain white supremacy in the aftermath of the Civil War. The group's name is derived from the

Greek word for "circle." The Klan's symbol is a burning cross, which represents their belief in white supremacy. The KKK has been involved in many acts of violence, including the lynching of African Americans and the bombing of black churches.

In recent years, the Klan has been reduced to a small fraction of its former size, but it remains a dangerous and hate-filled organisation.

The Nazi Party

The Nazi Party was a political party in Germany that was founded in 1920. The party's leader, Adolf Hitler, rose to power in 1933 and led the country into World War II. The Nazis believed in a master race of blonde-haired, blue-eyed people and advocated for the extermination of Jews, Romani people, homosexuals, and other minority groups.

Under Hitler's leadership, the Nazi regime was responsible for some of the worst atrocities in human history. Six million people, (Jews and other minorities) were systematically murdered during the European WWII Holocaust. (There have been several other 20th-century holocausts, including Pol Pot's Khmer Rouge and, the Cambodian holocaust, killing 3 million people. Idi Amin in Uganda & Malawi, West Africa, killing 1 million. The 1975–1978 Indonesian invasion of Timor is estimated to have exterminated 600,000+ Timorese; and others)

The Nazi Party was eventually defeated in 1945 and disbanded shortly thereafter. However, neo-Nazi groups have emerged in recent years and continue to espouse the hateful ideology of the original Nazi Party.

ISIS / ISIL

The U.S. has been battling ISIS and its forerunners for over a decade; however, ISIS continues to endure and expand within and outside of the U.S. Yet, ISIS has only recently been officially categorised as a cult. According to Bruce Barron and Diane L. Maye, ISIS meets the criteria of an apocalyptic Islamic death cult. ISIS is trying to resurrect a medieval Islamic society under the rule of a caliph (Abu Bakr al-Baghdadi) whose word is unquestioned and final. Similar to other cults, ISIS has little tolerance for outsiders and believes they should be conquered, forced to convert, or killed. Not surprisingly, ISIS is in a high degree of tension with the dominant society, a trait that is consistent with cultic behaviour. E. Friedland, in his "Special report: The Islamic State." highlights that ISIS' long-term goal is *"nothing short of world domination."* Unattainable goals, such as world domination, are also consistent with cultic mindsets.

The vast majority of Muslim scholars and clerics denounce ISIS. Experts argue ISIS is not Islamic and that its leaders are using religion to advance a political rather than a religious agenda. Yet, ISIS meets the definition and criteria of an apocalyptic cult, whilst maintaining Islamic roots. Similarly, Christian cults, behaving in a distinctly unchristian fashion, derive their ideologies and origins from their Christian roots. It has been pointed out by C. Chapman, in his "ISIS: Un-Islamic or True Islam?" that *"...when the ideologues of ISIS spell out in great detail their scriptures, tradition and history, they find the Islamic justification for what they are doing, it's simply nonsense to go on claiming that ISIS has nothing to do with Islam."* Indeed, it is highly unlikely ISIS would have emerged, endured, and expanded in the absence of its Islamic roots.

Cult Check List

If we briefly look at its leaders from a narcissistic perspective, we might say that they are in it for power, glory, and adoration. However, this would be a simplistic way of viewing their actions and motivations. The narcissistic leader of a cult is usually not the only one with grandiose fantasies; the followers also buy into these visions and illusions. In other words, the leaders could not maintain their grip on power without the support of their followers. It is important to understand that the followers are not mindless zombies; many of them are intelligent and educated people who have chosen to buy into the cult's ideology.

The reasons why people join cults are complex and varied but usually involve some combination of dissatisfaction with their current life, feelings of isolation and loneliness, and a need for belonging and purpose. The Islamic State is a brutal, barbaric cult that has no place in the 21st century. Its leaders are power-hungry narcissists who are using religion to further their political agenda. The followers have chosen to buy into the cult's ideology. If we are to defeat ISIS, we must first understand why people are drawn to its extremist and violent ideology. Only then can we hope to counter its appeal and stem the flow of recruits?

What is very interesting is that the criteria that Barron and Maye used to determine if ISIS is a cult are so similar to the narcissist checklist:

8. Charismatic leader
9. Authoritarian leadership
10. Exclusivism
11. Nonconformists
12. Totalistic organisation
13. Systematic indoctrination
14. Us-versus-them mindset
15. The ends justify the means
16. Aggressive proselytising
17. Money driven
18. Apocalyptic beliefs, strong
19. Exalted status
20. Islamic (Religious Authoritarian) based
21. Living leader centric
22. Lifestyle fosters isolationism
23. Membership exclusive
24. Preoccupied with expanding membership
25. Preoccupied with making money
26. Salvation, direct
27. Symbolism extensive
28. Theology dogmatic
29. Theology ritualistic
30. Milieu control
31. Mystical manipulation
32. Demand for purity
33. Cult of confession
34. Sacred science
35. Loaded language
36. Humans subordinate to doctrine
37. Dispensing of existence

Narcissist Check List

1. Charismatic
2. Authoritarian
3. Excluding
4. Nonconformist
5. Exercises absolute power over victims
6. Systematic indoctrination
7. Us-versus-them mindset
8. The ends justify the means
9. Aggressive
10. Money driven
11. Fear engendering
12. Sees Self as high-status
13. Claims Religious Authority
14. Self-centric
15. Isolationist
16. He sees himself as above most people and victims are privileged to be his victims
17. Seeks other victims
18. Drains victims of money
19. Narcissists are the only solution for their victims
20. Uses symbols and allegory
21. Dogmatic
22. Ritualistic
23. Brainwashing
24. Divine or Mystic
25. No one is good enough
26. Gaslighting -Loss of privacy for victims
27. Sacred science
28. Loaded language
29. Everyone subordinate to the narcissist
30. Often escalates to be life-threatening or a killer

Escaping the Cult

When individuals break away from the cult, they will be singled out, attacked and scapegoated. Nothing is off-limits. Adherents often find that the cult has kept a backlog of dirty secrets on them which they threaten to release. Being brutally discarded, threats, intimidation, betrayal, invalidation, humiliation and blackmail are not uncommon. Cults have even been known to orchestrate an exiting member's deportation back to their country of origin.

The worst abusers are often the vocal do-gooders, counsellors and those who have significant influence in their local church. Many argue that these people are so vicious, only because they are incredibly afraid of similar things happening to them. Therefore they lead the persecution charge, to draw attention away from themselves. This still does not excuse abusive behaviour. Whatever their reasoning they are practising a distorted and sadistic reality. The existing members must block these individuals out of their lives.

There are 3 simple steps to freeing yourself from a cult/narcissist:

1) No Contact

The first step is simply buying out of their false reality. It will feel like waking up as you remove yourself from the lies, manipulation and brainwashing. When you eventually want to break free of a narcissist/cult, it won't be easy to find people to help you.

YOU WILL FIND PEOPLE WHO WILL HELP YOU IF YOU REACH OUT.

Not everyone will be helpful. Some people WILL believe you and some will believe you are the crazy one and the narcissist. Don't reach out for help from other cult members. Don't try and save other members. Save yourself and get out. Continuing cult members will downplay your experiences and accounts and most will refuse to see the truth for what it is.

The best defence against a narcissistic cult is no contact. Stay as far away as possible and put your mental health first. They will never change or accept fault for their actions and will continue with their dysfunctional ways. Your first order of protection and safety is to have no contact with the narcissist/cult. This will preserve your sanity and aid recovery.

2) Build Your Self-Trust and Self-Esteem

You will be alone at first. This is a good thing you need to rediscover yourself. Don't panic and crave company or a new relationship. There is plenty of time for that. You need to focus on recovering yourself so that you can be a good partner and attract a good partner to you.

The last thing you need to do is to run into the arms of another narcissist/cult. Being alone does not equate to loneliness. You need to have some alone time so that you can hear your inner voice again, and remember your desires and joys. Silence and solitude are where you will find your peace and power.

3) Reach Out For Support and Help

Recovery cannot happen in isolation. You may feel like imposing self-isolation for a brief period however, you will need to reach out to others to fully recover.

Surround yourself with people who have gone through similar situations. You can find people who will resonate with you and validate your experiences. You know you have found a good support group, where they will authentically listen to you, and offer sound advice and resources to help in your recovery process. Most people that you encounter will have no idea of what is going on or what you have been through.

You will need to find a support group that specialises in helping people recover from cults/narcissistic abuse. It is always best to physically attend these groups. However, these days if you live in a remote area, there are lots of groups that are available online. Make sure you reach out for professional help.

The positive takeaway from all of this is that you have gained the skill to spot other cults, narcissists and toxic individuals straight away. Once you spot these you will set boundaries to protect yourself. Escaping the narcissistic cult will give you a sense of freedom, and inner strength.

As Charles Bukowski says: *"You may get burned for*

escaping and exposing the truth, but remember what matters most is how well you walk through the fire."

Stepping Out of Victim Consciousness

If you have been a victim of abuse you need to own it and stop letting the past hurt you in the present. Rise from your knees and never go down on them again and do what is necessary to never allow yourself to be a victim again. Live your strength. If you don't believe you're strong then fake it till you make it. However, this does not mean that you don't ask for professional help or seek out a support group or another recovered person willing to mentor you through your recovery. This workbook is my offering of mentorship, but you will need more. You need direct human contact with others who have rebuilt their lives and now thrive after abuse.

There is a difference between wallowing and or festering resentfully and being determined to recover by seeking the right help. Sick people need medicine to recover. Victims need staunch support. Humanistic psychology sessions or sympathetic friends can often make the problem worse rather than better. It can be like scratching the surface of an old wound that started to heal. All of a sudden you are reliving the pain and drama rather than healing. It can get you stuck in a loop of reliving the tragedy rather than moving forward. Sure you have to tell someone to get it out of your system. Choose someone for this who won't be burdened by your distress. Professionals are there for that purpose and they are trained to not take on others' stuff or let it get to them personally.

In short, recovery is about resolving to be recovered and strong. It's about seeking specialised professional help and support from others who have been down the same path as you and are now fully recovered. It's also about choosing your friends well and scrutinising your lovers and your behaviour with them. If they love you they will be patient, they will be genuinely interested in you and they will put the effort into creating closeness where your opinions and interests are valued and they will put the work into building a truly loving relationship that will foster growth in you and your offspring.

Echo survived. To do this she withdrew, decided to have a good life, make great choices and moved forward. Then she thrived. To do this, just like Echo, there may be times when you need to withdraw and disappear from the idly curious who are not seeking your recovery only seeking you out as entertainment. They like the wound to be fresh so that they get to enjoy every unsavoury moment. Even though Echo faded for a time, she returned and recovered but changed. She gave herself space and time. She faded from view but eventually returned to live a happy life. She formed a meaningful relationship with Pan and they had a happy pastoral life. However, in some versions of the myth, Echo's relationship with Pan is also abusive as he tries to have his shepherds tear her apart. In another version of this myth, she is adored by him & his shepherds love and worship her. She reset her mentor/parent figures. Zeus, Hera & Artemis were not the most loving of patrons, but Gaia was very tender. Surround yourself with tender people who truly care for you and support you. People who are willing to do things for you, not people who are demanding that you do things for them. Be gentle with yourself and you will attract people willing to be gentle with you. True recovery may take some time. Allow yourself the space and the time to heal. You will know you are healed when you look back on this time of your life as though it happened to someone else as if it was a distant myth. No longer a perfect fit for a Narcissist.

Survival Technique 8
Recognising Your Victim Status

Shame keeps many victims from admitting that they could have been foolish enough to have allowed themselves to get caught in an abuse loop.

The media tends to focus on pathetic weak women as victims. The truth is that many abused women are strong, educated and accomplished. Narcissistic abusers find these types of women much more useful, so the strong accomplished ones of a certain type are often targeted.

> There is NO SHAME IN HAVING BEEN A VICTIM
> only in the remaining one.

So now is the time to take a good, long, hard, honest look at yourself and your circumstances, to see how closely your patterns have begun to match the victim role. There are 2 parts to this technique. They flow into each other. When you do them you will see the flow.

> This is a process of self-examination. These exercises are not intended as a clinical diagnosis.
> This exercise is designed to get you to take a step back when examining your situation.

Honesty With the Self Through Myth

Sometimes it is hard to be truthful with yourself because you are used to giving excuses to yourself or others for your situation. But here's what I want you to do.

Go back to the section on the story of Narcissus and the story of Echo. I want you to imagine that Echo is your daughter as you re-read that short section. Imagine, as a parent, as a mother or a father, it is your job to help her and to defend her. Then answer the questions following in that frame of mind.

1. Your daughter Echo claims to love a boy called Narcissus who is very mean to her. What do you think causes Echo's feelings of love?

_____
_____
_____
_____
_____

2. Are her feelings real love?

_____
_____
_____
_____

3. Why do you feel this way?

_____
_____
_____
_____

4. Then why do you think your daughter Echo continues to love Narcissus despite being insulted, assaulted and rejected?

_____
_____
_____
_____
_____

5. How is she justifying her actions?

_____
_____
_____
_____
_____

6. Have you ever felt the same way that Echo does?

_____
_____
_____
_____
_____

7. If so, what words would you use to describe how you felt?

_____
_____

_____
_____
_____

8. Have you ever felt the same way that Narcissus does?

_____
_____
_____
_____
_____

If so, how did you act at that time?

_____
_____
_____
_____
_____

9. If you could go back and do it again how would you act now?

_____
_____
_____

_____

_____

10. Are you proud, ashamed or neutral in your feelings about how you acted at that time?

_____

_____

_____

_____

_____

The above should help you realise that you, respect others too much to dish out this kind of disrespect and abuse to others and would not tolerate the abuse that you have suffered happening to another. So why tolerate it towards yourself?

Why have less respect for yourself than you would for your daughter?

There are no right or wrong answers here. You are not wrong. Just look at your actions with eyes of awakening understanding.

Now close the book, meditate and rest.

We will examine your responses later in other exercises in this workbook and you may wish to share these with a skilled professional specialist or mentor. If you choose to keep these answers private that is perfectly OK too.

Identifying Your Victim Status

Think about how you have suffered. If you fall over and hurt your knee it is outwardly obvious, yet, things going on inside are not. We have to have a good long look at what hurts and where before we can understand how to treat ourselves for full recovery and how long it will take. So, in the following list please circle any types of hurt that you have suffered due to emotional abuse from a narcissist:

- Emotional
- Physical
- Sexual
- Spiritual
- Financial
- Psychological
- Mental

If you have circled more than one, please rate them from 1, being the greatest hurt to 7 being the least. These show the areas you feel have sustained the most damage.

Emotional abuse results from all of the previous forms of abuse. Physical abusers are emotional abusers. Sexual abusers are emotional abusers etc. It can also affect the way we interact with others. This is called interpersonal damage. This is a form of PTSD (Post Traumatic Stress Disorder), known as Complex PTSD. Complex PTSD results from abuse upon abuse, leading to serious emotional trauma. Victims develop a variety of coping mechanisms which can include:

- Dissociation.
- Addictions.
- "Deadness."
- Anxiety.
- Depression.
- Eating disorders.

- Loss of sense of self.
- Loss of sense of personal value.
- Loss of identity.
- Loss of the ability to trust your intuition.

Please circle any of the above that you feel may apply to you. If you have circled more than one, please rate them from 1, being the one you feel you have experienced the most to 10 being the least. Now refer back to your answers to 'Honesty With the Self Through Myth' questions 6 & 7. Have you used any of the words in this section in your answers to questions 6 & 7?

These questions show your areas of vulnerability. Any repeated emotions or experiences that scored highly, help to identify what damage you have sustained from your abusers. Please list in this space your areas of hurt, try to quantify that hurt, and, using words from the list above or your descriptors, describe your coping mechanism for that hurt.

_____
_____
_____
_____
_____
_____
_____
_____

_____

_____

_____

_____

This will help you establish how complex the damage is from your abuse.

Note that these score interpretations are self-examinations. They are not a clinical diagnosis.

Recovery Check List

Recovery from narcissistic abuse requires that you acknowledge that you have been a victim, and no longer wish to be abused nor to live in victim consciousness. You have to acknowledge that recovery means you working to heal yourself and to stop trying to fix your partner and make excuses for them. You are the only person that you can cause change. You need to heal YOU. Recovery from narcissistic abuse requires holistic healing; emotionally, mentally, physically, and spiritually. Recovery is a journey, a continuum, a process, not just a destination. For me writing this book and sharing my story to mentor others on their healing journey, is part of my ongoing process of recovery. To heal from emotional abuse you need to:

Get Away From Your Abuser(s)

If you are still living with your narcissistic abuser, YOU HAVE TO LEAVE. There is no waiting for them to improve. Regardless if it is your lover, spouse, parent, friend or boss. Your life is in danger. You cannot predict when their condition will accelerate or when their behaviour will deteriorate. Though their condition usually follows a pattern, there is no time scale as to when it can progress to Malevolent Narcissism and become life-threatening. You owe it to yourself, your dependents and your loved ones to protect yourself from further damage. You owe it to yourself to get out now. There are shelters and support agencies set up and designed to help you. Look in your local telephone book or search online. No house, bank account or any amount of material possessions is worth the damage this relationship will do to you. GET OUT NOW AND DO NOT GO BACK.

Get Help

When you move away from your abusive partner you are going to need a support network. Everyone needs a support network. Plan for it. No one can live in isolation in society.

Survival Technique 9

Honest Self Assessment of 'Assets' and 'Needs' Here and Now

Ask yourself:
- Do I need physical protection? Police? Family? Friends? Courts?
- Who can I count on to support me? Family? Friends? Community Aid? Work?
- What kind of support will I need? Emotional? Specialist? Medical? Employment? Spiritual? Basic?
- Have I got the basics covered? Food? Clothing? Shelter? Work? Finances?
- Do I need legal help? My solicitor? Legal Aid? Courts? Mediator?
- If you have children, will you need childcare and schools?

Circle what you will need above and make some more plans here and in your journal.

_____

_____

_____

_____

_____

_____

_____

_____

_____

If your narcissist partner has succeeded in isolating you from your friends and family, then you may need to turn towards government/community-supplied assistance. Unfortunately, spousal abuse is such a common, longstanding problem that every sizeable community has long-established shelters for the abused. They are not hard to find. A telephone directory, a search online or (depending on which country you are in,) a visit to the local police station or library can help you find these resources quickly. The Salvation Army is legendary for being able to provide such support in most Westernised countries.

Apart from your basic needs of food clothing and shelter, you will also have to get your emotional needs met. You cannot heal from emotional abuse alone, because it is a relationship injury. To heal from any type of relationship injury, you need people you can relate to. You can find abuse support groups in every sizeable community. Specialist narcissist support groups are becoming far more common with the rapid rise in this disorder. When I needed support 30 years ago it was hard to find any abused women support groups so I started my own. We would meet in a different home of one of the abuse survivors each week and we would each bring some food to share and discuss our survival. It was a friendly, happy, nourishing time where people who had not smiled for a long time suddenly found themselves laughing and relaxing.

I also needed child care, domestic help and handyman assistance. I decided to go back to university, something my husband would not allow. I found brilliant people to help me with these but I could not afford to give them enough work to support them. So I found them additional work and in no time it became a domestic service and handyman agency. I was a joint winner of Australia's Queensland Business Woman of the Year, with a business called "Rent-a-Man Rent-a-Wife," the first of the franchised domestic service agencies in Australia, all because of the need to create a support network for myself.

It is also vital that you find a good therapist who specialises in Narcissistic Abuse Recovery (NAR) so that you can work through some of the issues that you are exploring in this text. Process-oriented therapies like Gestalt Therapy and Voice Dialog work much better for most than humanistic psychology, which seems to keep the wounds fresh and open for much longer.

What can you think of to create support networks for yourself?

_____
_____
_____
_____
_____
_____
_____
_____

Personal and Immediate Resource Directory

List Support Contacts

Make a list of all the possible contacts you will need to recover. Names and phone numbers. Here's the hard bit: You will need to give them a good old-fashioned phone call, not an email or a text. The message is in the medium. People take it far more seriously if you have taken the time to phone them and you will get far more comfort and support if you can hear their voice and expression.

Don't announce anything about your relationship on Facebook or other social media. It makes you vulnerable and a victim. Randoms don't need to know your business and it makes you look desperate for sympathy to those who don't know you very well.

Supportive Friends or Family Members

Remember that your ex may have turned a few of your friends or family against you. Don't waste your energy on these people. This has been a good test of friendship for you. Remember "A friend in need is a friend indeed." The rest will get it when they fall victim to the narcissists themselves. Then it is up to them if they will put in the effort to be forgiven by you -

Think for now ... Who is your BEST support?

_____
_____
_____
_____
_____
_____

Local Police Domestic Violence Unit

Put 911 / 000 on your speed dial even if there has not been any physical abuse till this point. Phone and make an appointment with your local domestic violence liaison officer (You may be surprised to find one even in a small town) They generally appreciate knowing preemptively that things could become an issue, even if it is remote. Even if they say officially, they can't do anything, they often mark the address for immediate response to watch for a while. Additionally, they have access to resources. They can often recommend free counselling, support groups, financial assistance, child care and other useful things. Give them a call as soon as you can.

_____

_____

_____

_____

_____

_____

A Professional Counsellor or Volunteer Professional

Okay so you're not the narcissist, so why do you need a counsellor? Because whether or not you realise it, you are suffering from Post Traumatic Stress. You need to talk it through with someone who has seen this and helped other people recover from being the victim of a narcissist. This is not a job for your family and friends. They have patterns of behaviour with you and they won't know what to do. How to be what you need. This is a kindness to them, as there are details that friends and family don't want to hear or need to know.

This person can be a trusted religious minister if they have had experience helping people recover from narcissistic abuse and as long as they are not a minister of a cult-style belief system. A defining factor of many cults is that they employ similar victimisation and bastardisation techniques as individual narcissists.

If you don't know a professional counsellor near you, then google one close by your location and phone their office

_____

_____

_____

_____

_____

_____

Work: Colleagues & Bosses

If your living circumstances have changed and it may affect your work you should let your work know. Some larger employers have health funds that they pay into, to help their staff through such times. You may be entitled to some time off for a change of circumstances. You must let your boss know if you work with your partner, as they will be able to monitor if any narcissistic games get played at work, or they may move one or the other of you to a different location preemptively. Your workmates may be surprisingly supportive. But gauge who to tell details to. Not to your ex's friends and don't share too much with your boss if they are a bit of a narcissist themselves. If you are living in rental accommodation you may need to tell your landlord that they have moved out or to change the locks.

Boss

_____

_____

Colleagues

_____

_____

Landlord

_____

_____

Child Care

Did you rely on your partner for child care? Who can help you with that right now? I went back to university after my life changed on a government incentive for single mothers, in which they provided free child care next to campus. For a few extra dollars my sitter, Beau, who became part of the family, also cared for the kids whilst I worked part-time. You may be surprised who will, even temporarily, help out till you can hire someone

_____

_____

or

_____

_____

You will always need a backup.

Food - Clothing - Shelter

Narcissists often manipulate circumstances where even powerful people no longer have income or anywhere to go. Once they are completely dependent upon them and they feel their partner can't leave, then the abuse starts in earnest. However, these days there are many organisations set up to help recently separated parties and their children fleeing from abuse. A good first stop, and one that I can personally recommend is the Salvation Army. When I left the father of my second child, I retired to my hometown with nothing. My father found me a small cheap flat with a wonderful South American landlord. Mr Pasquale lived on-site and always kept a protective eye on me and my two boys. I felt safe. However, because my father was then a member of the Jehovah's Witnesses, he was ordered to not have anything to do with his "worldly daughter." The organisation, I was raised in, follows a narcissistic abuse pattern which was ingrained into me as normal behaviour. It haunted me for the early part of my adult life. Repeating a pattern of narcissism in three relationships. Two personal and one working. However, from day one, the Salvation Army showed my children and I, extreme compassion, with regular food parcels, beds for us to sleep on and a huge bundle of toys for my children, as it was Christmas time. One of the brand-new stuffed toys was bigger than me. My youngest son's eyes got so big in his little face when he saw it, I cried with joy. To me, the six-foot-tall white dog with an elongated neck and short legs was a universal sign. The moment it came to the door, on the 2nd day of our new independent existence, I knew I would have a job soon and that we would be OK. The Salvo's were amazing and, in gratitude, I still donate to them today. They have helped many victims begin to rebuild their lives. Don't be too proud to ask for and receive help with necessities if you need it. What aid organisation(s) is near you, just in case?

_____

_____

_____

_____

_____

_____

Legal Representative or Legal Aid

Narcissists love to threaten people with court. Don't let them catch you on the back foot with this one. Be ready. There is nothing wrong with being prepared. Who can help you legally?

_____

_____

Do you need pro bono? / Legal Aid?

_____

_____

Implement Self-Care

Incorporating self-care into your daily routine is a positive first step toward recovery from Narcissistic Abuse.

Breathe

We hold our breath when we are under stress. Any time that you become conscious of stress, feel overwhelmed or panic, take 10 long slow deep breaths. Breathe in deeply through your nose. Fill your lungs with as much air as possible. Breathe out through your mouth, visualising that you are breathing out the stress and tension that you are feeling. Visualise it leaving your body as a dark cloud that rapidly dissolves in the sunshine. You can pause for deep breaths at any time and anywhere. You will find that this will help regulate your emotional state. Thirty years ago when I started teaching these techniques, there were no mindfulness apps, nor any fitness watches, that remind you to stop and take a deep breath. We would tie bits of red string to our fingers and wrists so that each time we went to do something with our hands, we would see the red string and pause for 10 deep breaths. This is still a very good technique and in many ways far more effective than app notifications that can be easily ignored.

Be Creative

What do you do that is creative? Being creative is a great way to retire and channel the experiences you have been through. Write them down. Draw, paint, scrapbook, adult colouring or express them in any form of art or craft. But your expressions of creativity do not need to be limited to the release of the negative. We all have something in us we need to bring into this world and share with others. It could be starting a new business, going to dance classes or playing with your grandchildren. Look for opportunities that inspire creativity. When you create, you grow. When you grow, you heal and recovery begins. Schedule the time below to play, create or dance!

_____
_____
_____
_____
_____

Change You Self-View

You are so much more than you think you are. Thinking of yourself as a victim keeps you in a victim role. Change the way you see yourself. All of the exercises will help you to begin to change how you view yourself. You have been a victim in the past but that is not what you are going to be in the future. In your journal make sure to note any positive changes that you notice about yourself, your growth and your recovery. In your journal write a few words about how you ideally would like to see yourself in the future and how you would like your life to be.

_____
_____

_____

_____

_____

Something Fun for You To Do on Your Own or With a Friend

There are going to be times when you will just need to dehyperventilate and destress. A little planning can make this a regular and pleasant part of your life. Joy is the fastest thing that will move you towards full recovery. What makes you Joyful? A picnic, beach or hike in a national park is free and a great stress release. What are some things that are fun cheap and easy for you to do with a friend or your children?

_____

_____

_____

_____

_____

A Spoil or Pamper Thing for You To Do When You Are Feeling Stressed or Deserve a Reward.

Ok, something you may want to spend a little money on. Go on, be spontaneous and plan for it! A picnic, a facial, a massage, a yoga retreat, a trip away, a nice meal out, a night on the town. What is something you can do that will make you feel special and joyful?

_____

_____

_____

_____

_____

Detox from Abuse

Here are a few things to begin straight away that can start to clean your mind and soul of toxic narcissistic residue

Detox From Toxic People

- *Create Boundaries*: Be aware of the people, activities and responsibilities that no longer serve you. It takes time and energy to create and maintain relationships. Your time is precious. It is something that you can never regain. Why put energy into people that are toxic to you? Choose wisely who you will spend your most precious commodity with, and walk away from those who drain you. If you cannot because of work etc. then you must draw your line in the sand. Allow those people information about you on a need-to-know basis only and do not socialise with them. Especially, if they are trying to push their way into your life. Additionally, When you establish boundaries you are reinforcing healthy self-esteem.

- *People can be toxic*. You would not knowingly swallow poison. You would not eat rotting or toxic food. Then, why allow poisonous people into your life? Some people who are in your life to nourish you can be annoying. We are not talking about annoying people. Make a list of people in your life that, by their behaviour, make your life worse, not better. People who leave you feeling drained or shaken.

_____

_____

_____

_____

_____

Now ask yourself why those people are still in your life

Write Your Feelings in a Journal

If you haven't bought yourself a journaling book to go along with this work book Stop! and go and get one now. I recommend making it an attractive book that you want to pick up look at and hold each day. Believe me, it is worth spending a couple of extra dollars on this. Keep it specifically for notes about your recovery. Take a few minutes to jot down whatever comes to mind. Before bed, it will help you sleep. In the morning it will help you get organised. You can write everything in if from phone numbers of supportive friends, removalist details, doctor's appointments, notes for direction of your solicitor, and court dates. It is most important for you to write down thoughts and feelings as they occur to get them out of your head so that you don't keep going over the same thing. There are no thoughts too insignificant, too dark or too embarrassing. You will never have to show this to anyone else unless you choose to share it with your therapist. This process allows you to acknowledge what is on your mind and what you are feeling. And to keep a record of where you are at. Remember to place a date and time next to each entry.

Exercise

Exercise shows that you care for your physical well-being. It will improve things for you. It makes you feel good because it triggers the release of your endorphins. It can be your time out if you exercise alone. It can be your social time if you choose to exercise with others. You don't need to go to all the expenses of a personal trainer, there are lots of meet-up groups for walking, boot camp, hiking, dancing yoga and standup paddle boarding. Choose something you enjoy, then it will be easy to commit to your well-being. The better you feel physically, the quicker your recovery will be. Make a plan below to begin a simple form of exercise each week.

_____
_____
_____
_____
_____

Diet

Mental and emotional health challenges can often result in poor food choices. A poor diet can spiral us down physically and make recovery hard. A healthy diet fuels natural energy and boosts our self-esteem and confidence. Spoil yourself with an appointment with a nutritionist. Below list the healthiest things you ate today. (And No! Diet Coke is not a health food)

_____
_____
_____
_____
_____

Meditation

There are lots of free meditation groups. It is worth the effort to go along to a good one. When you are recovering from emotional abuse it is best to try to locate a non-denominational group. Meditation will help you clear your mind, increase concentration, reduce your stress, lower blood pressure, and reset your mood and your attitude.

_____

_____

_____

_____

_____

Mindfulness

is the practice of being aware of, and in the present moment. It is far too easy as a victim to rerun scenarios out of stress anger and curiosity if things could have been different somehow. This will keep you stuck in the past and not allow you to move forward towards recovery. Mindfulness occurs when you slow down to notice the sensations of what you are experiencing right now. Light a candle and enjoy the scent, colour and feel of the candle wax. Notice the sound of the striking match. Watch the vapours rise from it as you put it to the wick. Notice where the flame starts, the colours in the flame the heat shimmer above it. Notice which way the wick curls as it burns. Try to see the centre of the flame where there appears to be no flame at all. You have to be very present in the moment to notice all these things. Mindfulness is about being firmly rooted in the present. There are a plethora of mindfulness apps with a variety of exercises that you can set to happen for a minute every hour. Many workplaces are encouraging the use of mindfulness apps on the computers of their workers. What are your favourite mindfulness exercises?

_____

_____

_____

_____

_____

Limit the Use of Technology

Have technology-free days where you don't watch TV or the computer. Try to do this once a week. Technostress has become a real thing. It is the antithesis of mindfulness. With the popularity of internet-connected smartphones, it seems everyone is distracted 24/7. Being constantly connected can lead to a frenzied state, drawing your attention away from the present. Changing your usage habits with technology can have a substantial impact on lowering anxiety. Try to avoid looking at your cell phone first thing in the morning and establish a cut-off time at night. Write a technology-free schedule for yourself below noting be times and daytime hours that are tech-free.

_____

_____

_____

_____

Sleep

How well are you sleeping? Shakespeare said it's *"Sleep that knits up the ravelled ends of care... Balm of hurt minds... Chief nourisher in life's feast."* (Macbeth: Act 2, Scene 2) If you are not sleeping well then let's try a sleeping protocol.

- No coffee, caffeine/guarana lifestyle drinks, or other stimulants after dinner.
- Shut down the TV, mobile phone, tablet and computer at least one hour before bedtime.
- Don't read horror novels or things that raise anxiety before bed.
- Meditate and listen to soothing music.
- Make your bed a pleasant place to be. Keep your bedroom reasonably tidy and wash your bedding frequently. Keep the room cool, so that you want to snuggle up and limit light pollution.
- Pets can disturb your sleep patterns so don't allow pets where you sleep unless they are assisting you to feel physically safe with the lights off.
- Drink mild herbal sedative teas about 15 minutes before you get into bed.

If you don't have a sleep tracker then write down below how you slept and what your pre-bed sleep routine was for 3 nights in a row.

_____

_____

_____

_____

_____

Thrive

Okay, so if you can do all of that you can do anything. You may not see it now, but you will. After you have been through this, there is nothing that life can throw at you that you cannot cope with. Whether it be a business opportunity, family situation or future stress if you work through it similarly to the checklist – you will find that you are breaking huge problems down into its component parts. You will be a valuable employee and able to tackle very big things in life.

As a bonus, there are a few more bits of self-care that you can implement that turn the act of thriving into the state of **"Thrival."** that's the state of being that is actualised, and way beyond just mere survival. Before you know it, you'll be living your best life, and nobody will ever be able to victimise you again.

Survival Technique 10

Share Your Personal Stories

One of the most important survival techniques is to share your story. Yes, you should find a group of people who have been through similar things that can be your support group. If you have not found that as yet, I encourage you to write down your story. Even if the story is only something for you. You do not have to show it to anybody else. You may wish to show it to your therapist or your group. But that is your choice there is no pressure for you to share what you have written with anybody else. But it is important to get it out from inside of you onto a piece of paper where it looks less threatening than it does rattling around the inside of your head and heart. Once it is there you can choose to do whatever you like with it. Whether that is to share it with people that you want to help or need help from. Or you can burn it and release the energy back into the universe. This act of creating your story and seeing it turn into smoke and heat is very cathartic. Releasing your story by sharing it, externalises it. Externalising what you have been through is the most important step that will prevent you from repeating your pattern and getting into another relationship with a narcissist.

I cannot stress how important it is to be consciously aware of narcissistic red flags when you enter into new relationships. We can become more aware of how to see these red flags by attending support groups or by finding someone with whom we can share our experiences. This would need to be someone who has been through a similar level of narcissistic abuse as you. You both don't need to be recovered, but it is good if at least one of you is.

The worst narcissist abuse was by my ex-partner Tony. His next victim, Jo-Ann reached out to me and we have been able to be a great support to each other. We have been able to share and completely understand each other's experiences, which are so similar because we had the same abuser. We can both see very clearly that these narcissist techniques apply to more than just one man. All narcissists have a very similar morphology and sociopathy. Recognising those patterns is vital to breakaway and recovery. Additionally, Tony tried to convince groups that we belong to, that we were the victimisers and that he was the victim. Therefore, by sharing our stories with our groups, we have been able to turn the tables on the lies he told about each of us. The fact that we both had the same victimiser has been a red flag to many others in these groups and saved them from much pain.

Here are our personal stories of Narcissistic victimisation by the same person, and our eventual recovery.

Shé's Story

My adoptive mother was a narcissist and a medicinal drug addict. She abused me physically, emotionally, mentally and sexually until I moved out of the house at seventeen. I still find it difficult to talk about some of the depraved things that she did to me as a child. After having been raised by narcissistic parents, in a narcissistic religion, that forced me to marry a narcissistic man, I should have been more careful. Yet, after leaving my husband and my religion, I began working for a narcissistic boss who set up a cult! I then had 2 more narcissistic relationships and finally broke the cycle after a lot of work on myself.

My life began to prosper. I was awarded Queensland Businesswoman of the Year. I completed psychological counselling studies. I opened my own centre/retreat and finally entered into a relationship with a very, tender, caring, partner named Rick. I was really happy. I had worked through my victim stuff for 10 years. I even ran meet-up groups and workshops for people who were victims of narcissistic abuse. Then my partner and I separated suddenly and amicably.

For a while, I was contented being single, and busy running my businesses and a charity. Then I went to a spiritual retreat and met the most narcissistically abusing partner of my life. Tony was a beautiful, blonde, bodybuilder, who looked like Dolph Lundgren. He and Dolf had known each other at university.

Initially, Tony was very sweet and polite. He was well-educated and financially secure. At first, he was very attentive. It was a long-distance relationship for two years. For two years, I would get charming phone calls most evenings for two hours. He lived and worked in Sydney. I continued to run my retreat on the Gold Coast,

1100 kilometres away. We would travel to be together twice a month.

He confided in me that his greatest desire was to write a book and have it published. I told him I could do that for him. I am sure that he knew that before he began the relationship, and that is why he began the relationship with me. We began running workshops together on Hermetics and compiling notes on the resultant experiences of the participants of our workshops. Initially, he did not understand what Hermetics were, or how these principles could be applied practically in people's lives. I was happy to teach him and treat him like an equal teaching partner in my workshops. He was my romantic partner, so why wouldn't I? I wanted this to be a partnership of equals. I didn't want him to feel any less than me. I introduced him to esoteric groups that I was working with within Sydney and Queensland. Eventually, we also ended up with a group in Melbourne as well.

After one year we had a commitment ceremony called a "Handfasting." This took place at the same annual retreat at which we had met one year before, in the presence of 300 other people. However, for some reason, which to this day remains obscure to me, Tony roofied me that night. He never explained why, nor did he ever deny it. I knew that Tony had been heavily into the drug culture at one stage before I met him. I later found out that he continued to be an avid user of bodybuilding steroids as well as combining them with amphetamines to keep him lean. It became apparent that this was an addiction cycle causing wild mood swings. Later we found out he was importing steroids and he lost his job at the airport because of this. I found out later that he had been paying a drug addict to steal rare books for him from exclusive bookshops, by paying for a single heroine fix for the thief, in return for the goods.

Tony later told me that his sister had been found dead in one of his units from a heroin overdose, even though she didn't take heroin. He gave me a very evil smile that chilled me. Tony hated his sister, still, I thought that this was an extreme reaction. After we were separated he would sporadically threaten me. One night, he told me that he had killed his sister. He was also implying that if I was a problem to him that's how people would find me, dead from a heroin overdose. I, like his sister, was a health fanatic and never took drugs, not even mild analgesics for headaches. During our time together Tony pretended to be vegan and would give himself B12 injections every day. He insisted on giving me B12 shots for my health. I could not help but think that if he had killed his sister the way he implied, that was how he had administered the overdose. I believe that the police did investigate this, after Tony had left the country to live in the US with Jo-Anne. However, too much time had passed since his sister's death and cremation, to find any conclusive evidence.

All of this came out at the end of our relationship. I may never have found any of this out if I had not lived with him. I did not intend to live with him in Sydney. He had spoken about getting a transfer to Queensland and moving in with me. It may have taken much longer to uncover all of this if I had not moved into his environment where he felt comfortable and had set up his control mechanisms. However, things changed suddenly. After two years, the lease on my property expired and my landlord wanted to substantially increase the rent. (by ten times!) I believe they wanted to try and take over my business but didn't realise, that I was the business. However, I could not afford to stay at that increased rate of rent. Tony hesitantly invited me to come to Sydney to live with him explaining that he had never lived in a cohabiting personal relationship before. I asked him if he was sure he wanted to do this, as it was a big commitment to move in with a woman who had two preteen boys. He reassured me that he wanted our life to continue together.

Things started to go wrong after moving in together. His bisexuality became more pronounced. He was spending more time with his gay friends in the showers at the gym and behaving more gay than straight. At the same time, he was flirting with more women, to the point where I began to suspect that he had been having affairs with several women, at the same time that he had been having a long-distance relationship with me. I had noticed some red flags previous to moving in but he brushed my worries aside. When I mentioned this to him he explained, that because of the way he looked, women would throw themselves at him, and he was only being polite to them. That he had had relationships with some of these women in the past and they found it hard to take "No" for an answer and kept pestering him. He reassured me that since we had met there had been nobody else but me for him. I now know that was a complete lie.

When we discussed having children together he said that he felt that I was too old, in my mid-thirties, to have a healthy child. That he would need someone much younger to have a child with. When I looked askance at him, he made out that he was only joking. Yet, I later found out that he had gotten a young woman called Sherrie pregnant, whilst we were together. Sherrie was a pretty, skinny, girl who worked on a community TV show. She had been a regular attendee at some of our events. She often came to my home uninvited. Other people had noticed Tony going off alone with Sherrie. One lady, Ambrosia, even caught them making out behind some petrol bowsers, whilst I was refuelling. He said that Sherrie had kissed him and that he did not expect it, and he had told her not to do it again. It was such a flimsy lie.

Every time I backed away from the relationship because of red flags, he came forward and tried to make things up to me. He'd even throw himself down on his knees and kiss my feet and beg my forgiveness. But it was just an act that only lasted an hour or so. Eventually, I realised that he just did not want me to move away before we had finished writing the book. More correctly, before I had finished writing the book for him.

While I was moving out, he found my computer, downloaded the book, and then jammed a screwdriver into what he thought was the hard drive. Fortunately, my old computer had an old floppy drive that was hardly ever used and all he had done was destroy the floppy drive. The hard drive remained intact and the manuscript for the book that he later had published solely under his name, is still on that hard drive with all the meta-data, showing I had written it and when I wrote it.

When I moved in with him all effort ceased. He never again said sorry for anything that he did. He never asked my forgiveness for his increasingly monstrous behaviour. His house, which we moved into, was not habitable. It looked like an insane person lived in this house. There was garbage piled in every room with a walking trail carved out to allow movement from room to room, between knee-deep rubbish. The bathroom was so black with mould that it looked like somebody had lit a fire in the bathtub. The wiring in the house smoked, the fences had fallen, and the back Veranda gave way underfoot. I was so horrified that he respected me so little, that he hadn't cleaned the house up for us to move into. I turned around on the doorstep, to walk away and find somewhere else to live. He grabbed me got down on his knees and begged me not to go. That was the last time he ever did that. When I stepped over that threshold it all changed. He became another person, something much darker.

He put no effort into cleaning up the house, so over the next month I spent all my time and effort cleaning the house, renovating it, and making it habitable for myself, my two children, and my two Great Dane dogs. The house went from being dingy and spooky to being open light and airy. I established an organic veggie garden in the backyard. I fixed the kitchen shelves the stove and the oven. I added shelving, rewired the whole house and landscaped the front yard. I painted the house and laid the new carpet myself. I essentially put a whole new floor on the house by creating a huge attic room in the roof space as a retreat for the children. The value of the home went up by $200,000 due to my renovations. I now know that is why he moved us into that dump. He needed that property renovated and he was happy for me to spend my money and time doing it. He knew I could. He had seen how I had restored my beautiful 10-room, 168-acre centre in Tallebudgera Valley. He saw me fix it up and the landlord ejected me when it was done and the lease expired. He planned to do the same with his derelict property all along.

From the moment that I moved in, the verbal assaults on me were constant. Nothing that I did was good enough for him. No matter how hard I tried, he always wanted more or better. The manipulation had started in full. He did not help with any of the renovations. He always made sure he was out of the house while I was working on things with the tradesmen. Initially, I thought Tony was on edge and cranky as this was the first time he had cohabited with anybody and now he had me and workmen in his living space. I was a little bit too willing to make excuses for this bad behaviour. But it kept escalating. He didn't just lose his temper with me at home he would do it in public places as well. Tony berated and threatened me so badly, walking home on the street in Hurstville, that a tiny 4-foot-tall, Asian, Jesuit priest, bravely jumped in between 6ft4 Tony and I. He stared him down and told him that that is not the way to treat a woman, or his partner it was not the way to treat any other living being on this planet. I had never really liked the Jesuit organisation before this but after this, my opinion of them went up one hundred percent. That young man was very brave and he stopped Tony mid-escalation in a public place. He knew what was going on, he had seen narcissistic victimisation in public places before and was not afraid to stand up to him. Narcissists will often back down when public opinion turns against them. On this occasion when Tony realised that people in the street had gathered around behind this young priest and were staring at him and were willing to back the priest up, Tony did back down.

There were many occasions like this within those first two months. At the gym, in taxi cabs or with other people driving us around. He didn't mind escalating in public places or in front of others if he could create a scene where he thought he was painting me as the bad guy, even though this never worked out for him. The public doesn't like seeing a woman being monstered by a large bulky man. I don't know how he could convince himself that public opinion was on his side. Even though he'd later try to claim that it was.

The first time that I realised Tony was a narcissist, was when we were on a train. He asked me to do something that I refused to comply with. I don't even remember what it was that he asked me to do. He snuck his hand under that bag on my lap, so that the people we were travelling with could not see. I thought he was going to hold my hand as a gesture of reassurance to me that he loved me, even though we disagreed. Instead, he dug his fingernails into my arms so hard that chunks of flesh were ripped out as I pulled away in shock and pain. It was like alarm bells, gongs and warning lights flashing and going off in my head at the same time. I felt so stupid that I had been so blind to this being another narcissistic partner. I stood there holding my arm with blood running down it. Our friends looked at me and asked: "What happened? What happened?" I couldn't believe that they couldn't figure it out. Tears welled up in my eyes and I could not speak. I just shook my head and got straight off the train as it pulled up at the next stop. I turned around and I went home and started packing to move.

Tony arrived home not long after me, yet in that short time I had packed so much already. I had quickly thrown things into boxes and suitcases, he could see that I was determined to move out. I could see by the look on his face he was not expecting this. There was not a sorry, no apology, he walked in like nothing had happened and started being very playful and charming. I was stunned, so shocked I could not move. Yet, before I realised it he had me laughing and joking along with him. "Where do you think you were going? You don't have anywhere to go. And you don't have any money left to move out. Where do you think you can go?"

"Don't you worry about that," I said, "I'll find somewhere." He did not know that somebody had already offered me the downstairs of a house in Castlecrag on Sydney's North Shore. It turned out to be a saving grace. One thing I had learnt in previous narcissistic relationships was to always have a plan B. Whether you are in a relationship with a narcissist or not, it is always good to know if there is a friend who is willing to offer you emergency accommodation, as life can always throw you a curveball. Planning for a 'Plan B' is a very sensible life skill.

Tony told me he did not want me to leave, yet he still did not apologise. I told him that what he had done was not how you treat people you want to stay around. I told him that I refused to be treated that way. He replied with THE core narcissist belief, "If you love me I can treat you however I like." I just replied "No you can't" and kept packing.

He had a story ready to 'explain' his behaviour. I made the mistake of listening to the excuse. He was sucking me in as I still wanted to discuss what just happened on the train and he could tell that I did. I told him that if he wanted to treat people that way then he needed to find somebody who wanted to be in a sycophantic, willingly submissive, bondage and discipline relationship with him and that is not what I wanted. This led to a discussion about love and surrender. Sometimes you let your partner have a win to show them how much you love them. If you can disagree agreeably, surrender was very different to being a submissive victim.

He explained that he had no idea what surrender was in a relationship. He had heard that love was surrender, but he felt that to surrender in a loving relationship was to lose. He said that he did not understand the difference between surrender and submission. He said he did not know how to learn that. I responded to his playfulness, by suggesting that if he wanted to learn it, then we should participate in a bondage and discipline session. Tony said that he had never had that kind of sex before and was very interested in it and what he could learn from it. This did not surprise me. Generally, men are interested in any kind of sexual foreplay that they haven't tried before. Tony was so successful with this verbal tactic that it disarmed my defence and completely distracted me from packing and moving out that night.

Two days later, we completed preparations for an evening of fun. Tony wanted to be tied up but soon had a very bad reaction to being restrained. He called his SafeWord very quickly. The session ended and I released him. The moment that he stood up he king hit me in the back of the head from behind with a closed fist. I went down to the ground. I have a vague memory of him kicking me several times. What happened for the rest of the night is still very blurry and I have not regained my full memory of that evening. At some point, Tony must've picked me up put me in the bed and left. I suspect that if I had died from concussion in bed he would have tried to say that he wasn't there and didn't know how it happened. I woke with a terrible headache and an incredibly sore stomach. I went to the toilet and there was pink urine. Urine with blood in it. I got the kids to school and then I rang the hospital and an ambulance came to take me to the hospital. I didn't want to drive in case I did have a concussion.

At the same time, a policewoman from the domestic violence unit turned up and asked to come inside. She asked me if had I assaulted my boyfriend as he had been to the police station to make a complaint. The sneaky f#*ker was trying to be preemptively litigious. I was swaying on my feet and the room was spinning. She took one look at me and realised that I had been battered. She told me to sit down. She looked around the room and saw all the boxes that I had hurriedly packed a few days before, after the train incident. She grabbed my face and asked me to look her in the eyes, but I could not focus on her. She probed her fingers down my neck and then down the sides of my body, in a frisking kind of move, I flinched. She asked me to raise my shirt as I was holding my stomach. There were bruises all over my stomach and ribs. I was surprised there were so many bruises on me. I started to cry. I told her what happened and she said "..the bastard must've started kicking you when you went to the ground." She escorted me to the hospital. She made sure that I had a brain scan and was checked for internal bleeding. She made me promise that I would finish packing those boxes and move out. She made sure that Tony stayed away for the weekend until I had moved. Senior Constable Christina Ridley has remained a friend up to this day.

We had only lived eight weeks together and within a week of the physical abuse, the arm scratching and the bashing, I had moved out. I had at least learned not to tolerate anybody hitting you, ever. It had only taken eight weeks to escalate to that point. I felt if I had stayed he would eventually escalate to kill me. However, the abuse did not stop when I moved out. I tried to keep things amicable and private. But that is not the way that narcissists do things. Tony's increasing attacks on me could not be hidden from our group in Sydney, but our groups in Queensland and Melbourne had, for their benefit, been kept unaware of it. When I moved out, Tony went to Queensland for two weeks and told them all that I had attacked him. I suppose he believed that even if I didn't tell them what had happened in Sydney, some of our students/friends from Sydney would communicate with the Queensland mob and eventually tell them how abusive Tony had been towards me. So he started a new cycle of lies to try and cover for himself. Mind you he was a 120 kg bodybuilder. And I was only 50 kg at the time. The idea that a skinny little thing like me could have done him any sort of bodily injury, was laughable. But narcissists can be very convincing with their lies. He got so caught up with his lies that he then laid charges against me in the local Sutherland courthouse. Christina was there when I went to court. She presented my medical records and the judge threw the case out and told Tony that he would not have him playing games in his courtroom. The judge then suggested that I lay charges against Tony. I just wanted it to be all behind me so I could move forward. Later that week, Tony came to me and told me he wanted me to move back into his house. That he missed me and that he loved me. He was frightened that I would lay charges against him, and begin a claim against the house that I renovated. Yet that same week he began to try to poison my new landlady against me. He was also already involved with someone else. He was in the process of preparing another victim/servant. She was an author and editor, Someone who could also work on the manuscript for him.

Jo-Ann, Tony's new victim, lived in the United States. I heard about her from mutual friends. Nine months after we had separated, I saw her at the same annual retreat at which Tony and I had met. I realised who she was but I felt no resentment. I could only feel sorry for her. I found myself in a cafeteria queue behind her. So I introduced myself and I wished her well. I told her that I hoped Tony behaved better with her than he had treated me. She looked at me strangely without saying anything. So I said that Tony and my relationship had been good while it was long distance. However, now that Tony was going to move to the United States to live with her, I said that I hoped things continued to be good with them both. Jo-Ann looked a little bit surprised, but she was gracious. I think she realised that I was being sincere and certainly was not being malicious. I did not hear from Jo-Ann or Tony again for 10 years. And then Jo-Ann came up on my friend's requests for my Facebook page. Our first internet chat made me realise that she had been suffering severe narcissistic abuse at Tony's hands for the whole 10 years. She finally dared to reach out. Here is one of the first conversations that Jo-anne and I had when we reconnected.

Jo and Shé Support Each Other

We were able to give support to each other. I cannot express how important it is to find people who know what you have been through. Other survivors can become your comrades as you begin to move forward again. We want to see each other succeed, fully recover and thrive.

Jo-Ann - Shame plays a huge role for victims. Speaking out and letting victims know they are not alone helps pull back the tide of shame that we should never have felt, to begin with. It's not our shame. It's theirs. They should be shamed by us all. Everyone needs to not let abusers feel they are safe to be abusive. Supporters of abusers should also be shamed as they are co-abusers.

Shé - Yes you have nothing to be ashamed of. You have all of our support. Well, you have all of the sensible people's support. You will find the ones who side with him have an insane unrequited crush on him. He will stop associating with the ones who know he has behaved badly and say so. (He stopped associating with all of our group in Sydney who witnessed his rapidly declining behaviour and did not approve. They all turned up to help me move out and were very supportive of me. Love and blessings to them all.) He will hang with the ones who know but will help him perpetrate a lie, and the ones who continue an association with him and then attack you, show that they are no better than he is and are just as happy to be women abusers too.

J - Yeah I've already had the kind that have an insane crush on him tell me:
"Oh, yeah. I know you two are having issues, but he takes such pretty pictures with me."
She's an owner of a shop for f*#ksake. Claims to be a priestess haha of a tradition that reveres the feminine divine. Right... Smh.. BFS. They must really love him more than their spirituality or whatever the f#*k they think they're calling it, cuz you can't revere the divine feminine and support an abuser of women.

S - Question for you: Did he make you spend all your money? He completely emptied my bank account on renovations to his home to make it "bearable for him with my children." I turned the attic into a second-floor retreat for the boys. I re-did the bathroom and added heaps of extra storage, all this is in two months mind you. (I know. Da! me) plus it was so run down that it needed major work to make it liveable. - The back veranda gave way underfoot, the wiring was smouldering if you turned on switches in some rooms and the fences had all fallen. It was so friggin' filthy! Then when I had done all of that and was running low on cash, he insisted that I buy my own food and water for the children and myself as his organic stuff cost too much to waste on "others." When finally he hospitalised me with what is now called a coward's punch, I didn't have enough money to move out so had to take emergency measures. But I did get out and I'm happy, very, very, happy now and more importantly, I am still alive!

Denise - (Is from Australia, formerly of our Brisbane group. She was supporting JoAnn on the internet and helped to connect us) OMG She DMontford, I had never realised it was that bad either until I talked to Jo-Ann Byers, about her experience and then realised that it must have been the same for you. Her story sounded similar to yours, except for the fact that it was him, that was doing all the work, spending all the money etc. :-(

J - Yes our experiences with our common abusive ex is practically exact in every way. It is frightening and at the same time comforting to share our experiences with each other. She has become such a source of strength. 🖤

Denise - That's awesome Jo, cos the abusers always want to put the blame on you and tell everyone different stories.

S - Denise, I didn't realise that anybody would believe him over me. I was the victim. Tony tried to lie about the abuse once on an internet group and we just rolled out the court transcript and Tony dropped it. He went silent and disappeared from that group. Wow, about paying for things that's a newy -Everyone knew I had paid for everything up here, flying him up and down. All they had to do was to think about it logically. I sold up everything, all my antiques everything. I was in a 10-bedroom house, I had a good job, plus the writing, plus the consulting work. I have no bad habits. I don't smoke, I don't drink, I don't do drugs. So where did all my money go within 2 months of going to Sydney? What I did hear, was that he claimed that the book and the hermetic ceremonies were his. Yet, everyone up in Qld knew we were working on a book and Tony was always joking that he didn't have time to write, so he was leaving it up to me. Besides I had been doing the workshops for years before he came along. I had been running workshops and writing for decades before him, and I thought most people in Qld knew I wrote all the ceremonies and kept all of the feedback because they sent them to me after each gathering.

In fact, I remember a few people went crook on him for the way he behaved in the ceremonies, acting like he owned them when he didn't write them. At Ra's house, I think, or it might have been the woman who had the shop at Cleveland when we were doing workings at her place. Very few people (except the nutty ones like Simone and Paul -both of whom had sex with him) said anything differently to me and what the nutty ones said was so crazy I just discounted them. I felt people would seek me out when they got over the uncomfortable period of two friends breaking up. But, as often happens with any break-up, many never re-established contact. Then I realised when a few of my friends started to ask about what had been said, and what had happened. I could not believe what I was hearing and how gullible people in Qld had been.

You know I have never been big on justifying myself in public - I have always thought "What other people think of me is none of my business" and if they want to think horrible things about me, then they were never really my friends! ;)

J - That is so right. The things that he had said about you Shé were so insane and so opposite of who you are. I know that he's doing the same thing about me. I don't care. Everybody here who knows me will know the truth and that's all that matters.

S - That's exactly right Jo!

J - Over $82,000.00 I spent on putting a roof over his head food in his stomach clothes on his back. Books he wanted. Travel to events and hotels etc. Every cent was invested into a future he never planned on sharing with me. I fronted everything for him.

S - Yep - you fitted

J - When he realised my money went dry and he had to start paying for his shit, man did it get bad.

S - He sees kindness and love as a weakness to be exploited, not as a gift to be grateful for.

J - It's actually sad that he will actually never know what it's like to be loved.

S - He knows he just doesn't care. Don't you dare feel sorry for him!

J - You're right... My empathy got the better of me for a moment.

S - Think about it Jo-Ann, his abuse of us and others, including his own family, is financial and status-driven. Here we have a very wealthy man, who won't spend a cent of his own money and is resentful of those who help him, seeing those who believe him as fools. These are words from his own mouth. How can you feel sorry for that????

J - It terrifies me what he has done to his mother and sister... it's no wonder his grandfather hated him.

S - And you know he is laughing at the ones who believe him. He said to me he could not believe how easy it was to get "Stupid people" (his words not mine) to believe the craziest lies about others. The crazier it is, the more people will believe it, He told me that himself. I saw him use it on his mother, then he used it on me. We both caught him out one day, telling each of us lies about the other. He didn't apologise - he just very matter-of-factly, stated the above. Like we should be glad that we were not foolish enough to believe him. He was shocked that I did not approve of this kind of behaviour towards others and I told him that it made me feel sick that he thought that his revealing this to me would fall on sympathetic ears. He saw his behaviour as an evolutionary mode of moving forward in the world. I told him I saw it as cannibalism and saw it as something I had to help him to get over. He didn't want to get over it. He doesn't want to get over it. -HE DOESN'T- He then used that against me, pretending he wanted to overcome it. We even went to counselling and the councillor told me to give up, saying words to the effect of: "....he's very intelligent, he knows what he is doing and he won't change." The counsellor reassured me there were only two courses of action, go along with him or get out fast. The counsellor felt that Tony's revealing his motives to 'ears unsympathetic to his motives,' showed that he felt above being judged by anyone and that he could do what he liked. That he was escalating and could make him react life-threateningly and violently towards me. And it did, very soon after that.

PLEASE NEVER FEEL SORRY FOR HIM Jo-Ann, not even for a second. Alarm bells, not sympathy!

J - Omg.. I'm so sorry Shé. He is such a monster... 😡 it makes me sick to think about him, and all that he has done to you and me and every person who bothered to care about him. He will continue to do these horrible things to people too. 😢

It is not far-fetched to see narcissists as potential killers. Here's how to break this situation down. Tony's extreme narcissism is a defence against feelings of inferiority. The person dons a mask of arrogant superiority in an attempt to convince the world that he or she is special. Tony has moral superiority syndrome, which is a form of narcissism. You can't argue with him. If you do, you will feed his narcissism. You are better off ignoring them or literally leaving them alone. You have to think of people like this, as drug addicts. The rush is an emotional chemical, released in the brain by being a victimiser. It becomes addictive, something they crave. Drug addicts always need a bigger fix, a greater rush. He needs targets to release his feelings of being inadequate by making him feel superior. When you engage, he feels like he can dominate you, which makes him feel powerful, and suppresses his feelings of low self-esteem. Eventually, this escalates their behaviours. Like the psychologist warned, killing is the eventual step. If he has already killed, like he has claimed, then the risk of a recurrence is great.

Jo's Story

Jo-Ann has a longer history of life-threatening narcissism. Her story highlights that the morphology is the same for each victim. It shows that the abuse techniques are the same for each victimiser, even though the intensity can vary. Here is Jo's story:

Mom

Sadly, my mother was severely traumatised as a young child growing up during WWII England. She was terrified of the Nazi aircraft and was once caught with her father, uncle and sister in the streets when a Nazi sprayed the street with bullets. Her father and uncle had to quickly grab the girls and shove them into a doorway to avoid being shot and there they stayed until the pilot finished circling back around spraying the street several times. There are many more terrifying stories of such close calls that would be traumatising to anyone.

While this does explain how she became a manipulative, controlling sociopath, it does not excuse any of her physical, mental and emotional abuse. It is unfortunate that even as an adult she refuses to see that therapy would be beneficial to her and everyone around her because in her mind she is just fine it's everyone else that is the problem.

My mother's family is Jewish and my father is Agnostic. Unfortunately, my mother refused to practice or see to it that any of her children were brought up within the traditional practice of Judaism. So I basically bounced around to different churches that my childhood friends attended and would invite me to go along to 'save me' until I was fifteen. My grandmother's sister, my great aunt, came to visit and began teaching me about her and my grandmother's practices in what some people now call Jewitch Craft. During the last few years of their lives, both she and my grandmother provided me with love, advice and instructed me, as best they could over the phone, into their practices.

There were many instances during my childhood when I was ignored, gaslighted, physically abused, severely punished for things I did not do, manipulated, deceived and so on. There are just so many, it was normal and I had no idea none of this was actually normal. Other children didn't get this treatment from their parents so I eventually thought I somehow deserved it. As a child, I could never figure out why, because no matter how helpful or good I was, nothing was enough.

Once when I was a teenager, I was on restriction to my parent's property lines. So I sat in the front yard and the neighbour boy Scott who lived two houses down and another boy who lived a few streets away in my track were riding their bicycles and stopped to talk to me. When my mother noticed she came out of the house screaming at me and the boys, then grabbed my ponytail and pain exploded in my head while she dragged me back into the house totally in pain-filled humiliation.

When I turned seventeen, I remember my mom believing I deserved her balling up her fist and hitting me in the face because I was standing up to her and not being an extension of her, wanting to be my own person. I was so stunned I just stood there while she walked away smug, thinking she had won. I went to my room and pulled my suitcase out of my closet and packed it with everything I felt I needed to keep with me. Mom caught me just after I zipped it up and burst into my room grabbed my suitcase while screaming at me, and locked it into her bathroom. So I left without my belongings as I knew I could not stay any longer.

My dad found me at my best friend's house crying. He listened to what happened and persuaded me to return, saying he would stop her from doing these things to me. Sadly he wasn't able to as he worked and she was a stay-at-home mother. So the summer after I turned nineteen she hit me again and I was done. A few days later I was on a plane to Hawaii, running into the arms of a young man who turned out to be a murderous psychopath.

Though I would like to be done with narcissists in my life, I feel I still have to deal with her, as my father's welfare is at stake. I have chosen to care for my invalid father, however, she wants me on call as her 24/7 slave. When I am there, she will pick any petty argument to give her the excuse to become a very toxic, nasty, horrible, person who says the ugliest things and slams any door, cabinet or drawer she can get her hands on to try to get more manipulate control over me. During the day when I cannot be there, she will even withhold the food I have prepared, from my dad and create an environment that is so negative you can slice it with a knife. I have tried to have her removed from being my father's carer but she is a master manipulator. She gaslights me to the authorities whilst being as sweet as pie to them. The authorities are unwilling to take action against "a little old lady." It is hard. I wish that governmental officials in these positions had mandatory training in recognising and dealing with narcissists of all ages.

To her, my life, and any future life I could have, is not important. She has determined that my only purpose in life is to ensure both my parents can pass from this life while living in their forever home they have lived in since 1969. If I dare try to have a life outside of her desires, she proves that she is still the same mother who dragged me by the hair, back inside the family property boundaries. These days she will use anything she can to disrupt my ability to accomplish any goals for myself and my future. Her main form of manipulation is messing with my invalid father's medications or serving him food that gives my father severe diarrhoea. She excuses her behaviour, by smiling evilly at me, whilst telling me that I should have been there to do this instead of her.

All I can do is try to counteract her and hope that she does not cause my father's premature death. Like most abusive narcissists she is accelerating toward taking a human life.

Keith

My earliest narcissistic relationship, other than my mother, was with one of my elder brothers. I had two brothers, but the eldest Stephen, who was my only protector, passed away when I was only thirteen years old and he was twenty-three. My other brother Keith who was six years older than I and the golden child would literally torment me and find ways to beat the crap out of me. He was both mentally and emotionally abused throughout my childhood and teenage years. My mother acted like an enabler and would just wag her finger at him and tell him he shouldn't do that... but of course that never stopped him.

His favourite thing to do, besides hitting me with his fists, was throw the heavy glass ashtrays from the 1970s across the room at me while I was distracted. I was supposed to duck. After the third time of being hit in different areas of my body including my head, I learnt to be on guard all the time. Never took down my guard before making sure Keith wasn't home.

It would not be until I was sixteen that I could stand up to him and end his horrible treatment towards me. You see, he had already moved out of our childhood home into his own apartment. One day he knew I would be home alone and came back for a 'visit' to beat me once again. His reason, he said, I hadn't gotten hit in a while since he doesn't live here anymore and he needed to make up for lost time.

Much to his surprise as well as myself, he ended up on the floor screaming because I had kicked him very hard in his testicles and I stood over him telling him to never touch me again or things would be worse for him. He ended up having to take himself to the hospital and have his testicles brought back out from inside his body.

I wasn't the last victim of his abuse, he ended up getting married and beating my sister-in-law too many times before she finally divorced him for his abuse.

The last time I heard about Keith beating another woman was when I was married, my family and I lived in a condo across from his. He was dating a sweet Japanese lady with two grown sons who owned a Sushi Restaurant. One night she called me after having locked herself in his bathroom for protection. She was crying hard and I could hardly understand what she was saying. I ended up just going over to see what was happening. Keith was raging and wanting me to leave… she was crying in the bathroom. I pushed my brother into a corner while yelling at her to get out of the house and go home.

I contacted her later and told her to take pictures and report his abuse to the police. Instead, she just moved away letting her sons run the restaurant in her place.

Sadly he hasn't learnt to stop blaming me for his problem despite me not having anything to do with him for 15 years or more. Narcissists always seek to blame somebody else for their actions and for the things that go wrong in their lives. They usually blame their victims. I was his first victim and always the first person he blamed. His most recent claim is the most ridiculous. Apparently, I am somehow responsible for him getting so sick he had to spend three weeks in hospital where he claims to have almost died. The fact that this was during the height of the Covid outbreak makes him want to blame someone even more as he couldn't have caught it by himself. Insanity.

If you're wondering, yes Keith is still my mother's Golden Child.

Todd

I met Todd while I was going to a local college to become a certified accountant. He was attending classes so he could go to university to study biochemistry. We saw each other in the quad and things took off quickly from there.

Todd came from a well-to-do family and he took me to nice places and spent a lot of time together when we weren't in classes or needing to study. He ended up transferring to Uni of Hawaii and that August was his birthday which is when I took a trip to visit and shortly after we were engaged.

One night after Todd had gone to work and then for a hike since he didn't have class the next day, he came home, I heard him arguing with someone so I went to the window in our bedroom. I saw he was arguing with my landlord who lived in the front section of the house we were renting. The next thing I saw was Todd pulling a machete out of the beach chair he was carrying and he cut off the head of our landlord. Things only got worse from there. I was forced to do horrendous things otherwise he was going to kill other people I cared about. For the next eight months, I lived a nightmare and things done to me I would never wish upon any living creature.

I was at his mercy and he had none. Eventually, the police found us. He was in the middle of making a deal with someone that was connected to human trafficking. The police found me tied up in the closet.

I will always have to worry if Todd gets out of jail. After having done everything possible to assist the police in prosecuting Todd for the murder, the courts gave him life but in Hawaii that only means forty years. During the first trial, I was shown a note by his defence attorney that told me he would kill me if I testified. I testified anyway. Ten years later I had gone through several years of therapy for what I endured and had started a family. I started becoming very paranoid and knew it, but could not help but feel like I was being watched and followed. So I went back to my therapist until one day I got a phone call from the Hawaii Prosecutor who told me that the courts had let Todd out on a technicality. He had been out and following me for 2 years before the Hawaii prosecutor called me insisting I testify again. I refused g because they could use my old testimony that's on record, but they took it to the California Supreme Court. The judge talked to me about returning to Hawaii and wanted to know why I didn't. I told him about some of the things that happened to me and how Hawaii didn't care and refused to allow any testimony of how I was also a victim. They had made up their minds and wanted to punish me. I was sentenced on trumped-up charges instead of being treated as a sexually/mentally/emotionally abused victim/ survivor of a psychopath.

The judge looked into the things I told him as to my treatment by the courts and did what he could and provided the protection of the State of California if I returned to put Todd back in jail. I had already fulfilled the requirements the State of Hawaii made me perform for the sentence I received, but the California Supreme

Court Judge made sure they could not trump up charges against me again.

Feeling safe is something I have never felt to this day. I will always wonder if he will make good on the message in his note.

Bill's Story

Let's just call me Bill. I am a retired, highly decorated military officer. I have an IQ of 164. I read, write and type in five languages. I have worked with a high level of intelligence and have seen some very dark sides of human nature, and did not think that I would be a person who would be easily manipulated, but I have been manipulated by systemic narcissism on a personal level. This systemic narcissism happens to men all the time. I would like women to be aware that it is not just women who fall prey to narcissistic manipulation. Hey, just ask Johnny Depp.

I have worked in Asian countries and have previously been married to a demanding and aggressive Japanese wife. But that relationship is very different to the situation I find myself in now.

I began a relationship with another Asian lady, 15 years ago. I met her in Thailand and eventually went to live in her village for some time to get to know her better. I checked out her background as thoroughly as I could and I became convinced that her affection for me was genuine. I have compromised a lot for love in my life and

I have always wanted to be loved genuinely in return. She appeared to ticked that box completely. I found her to be a happy, funny, hard-working person. She was a devoted Buddhist. She had a young daughter at the time. She said she was working hard so that her daughter could go to a very good Buddhist school. This was a great privilege and something that would give her family prestige. She presented as a person offering me the perfect loving family that would be devoted to me and never leave me. Initially, she was very attentive to me. She appeared to be loyal to me and jealous of me in a way that I had not experienced from any other woman before in my life.

I rapidly fell deeply in love with her. I adored her and I felt very protective of both her and her daughter. Whatever she wanted, she got... clothes, jewellery, houses, pets. Anything she wanted, I was happy to get for her. She had never experienced the luxury that I could shower upon her, and I was happy to do that. In my willingness to give to her, the power base shifted. Before I realised it, choosing my friends was part of what she wanted me to give her. Over a while, without my noticing, she began to drive wedges between my close friends and myself. Suddenly, I was isolated from all of my few surviving family and closest friends. There were various excuses... from her Asian Buddhist philosophy, through to the fact that she did not trust my close business partner and associate, sexually with her friends, even though some of her friends have been sex workers. I had become used to compromising for her so each increased level of compromise began before it was noticed. I now know that she pretended to be holier than thou, and morally outraged by the smallest moral transgressions. I now realise that she was manufacturing things that she could hold against my friends. I was told that if I continued to have anything to do with these immoral, unethical people whom I called friends, her devout Buddhist conscience would no longer allow her to have anything to do with me. Even though I was a good man, she told me that my friends would disgrace her daughter and her family. I understand enough about Asian culture to know that this is a thing. But it is a thing that is hardly ever practised in the 21st century. I was proud of the fact that she was so moral and upright and old-fashioned with old-world values. It made me trust her even more.

It was an interesting conflict of emotion. I was proud of her, yet, I was devastated, but felt I owed her because of the loyalty she was showing to me. It was surprising when the first one or two occurred. These were with female friends – devoted, loyal, long-term female friends, who were only platonic friends. I put it down to her feeling jealous and insecure. I felt I was protecting her by backing away from my female friends. Then she started to isolate me from my male friends as well. By the third one, I suspected there was something gravely wrong. Yet I was in so deep. I didn't feel I had an option. I had drastically changed my life to be with her. I had already sold my property and businesses in Melbourne, Australia, in preparation for moving to Thailand. My life was going to continue with her in Thailand. It was after we had arranged this that the selective isolation began in earnest. Yet, after selling up everything, it was hard to go back, hard to stop. I could not have remained in Australia and kept my friends – the only choice I felt I had was to isolate my friends and move forward to Thailand. I knew this would greatly change the life that I had. Moving to Thailand would make me 100% dependent upon her and her family. I felt a fear of being trapped as if I had no option. Yet her purported love and sincerity made me feel that everything would be alright. Love would make it all okay. She was a simple person from a simple culture living in simple black-and-white terms. After my complicated and convoluted life, I found myself craving a simpler black-and-white way. I agreed and moved ahead and found myself isolated from my friends and family. Even from my lovely, loyal, devoted daughter, Sandra. My partner had created so many personal conflicts with Sandra, that it became impossible for us to continue our father/daughter relationship with the closeness we had before.

My Australian life was gone so quickly – there was nothing left, except her plan of moving back to Thailand. I did go through a short bout of depression because of all of this. I felt like my life had imploded and destroyed itself. However, my lovely, devoted, Thai wife was right there beside me, being incredibly attentive and caring. No matter how cranky I got during this time, she was patient, telling me she understood, and how much she appreciated me changing my life to not bring shame to her family. During this period, I never doubted her love for one moment. The idea of moving to Thailand eventually seemed like it would be a refuge and a release for me. Initially, it felt like that.

Within 24 months of moving to Thailand, the reality of who, and what she really was, was unavoidable. When we moved back to her home village I learnt that she had several previous relationships with Westerners. She had worked as a hostess at various sex clubs, where she met these Westerners with the hope of putting this very plan into place. So much for her moral high ground.

I met several of her friends who had already done the same thing. They wore lots of gold. They took pride in letting themselves get fat and making their husbands follow meekly behind them. They made fun of their Western husbands in their native language, without him being able to understand. Deliberately shaming him to others. But I could understand Thai. I knew what they were saying. They never dared to say anything about me within my earshot. However, they would forget themselves, if they had too much to drink and start joking about their Western men, they would begin to boast how they had so cleverly isolated them, liquidated their wealth, and put themselves in a position, where they would be the only one legally entitled to it after he passed. They would mercilessly insult any women they knew who had been "stupid" enough to believe they had truly fallen in love with their Western husbands. My wife, as well as the others, stopped the act and let their guard down after they returned to Thailand.

The ultimate realisation came when I found that she still was married to a Thai man and the money that I had been sending to Thailand to support "her family" before we left Australia, had in reality, gone to him. He had moved to a neighbouring village before we arrived from Australia. I was never supposed to meet him while I was alive. But I am very good at finding things out. I just followed her one night, when she was going to the neighbouring village alone. After I identified her with him, it was easy to find out who he was.

I never thought it would happen to me. I thought I was too clever, too intelligent, too worldly wise. I have met many other Western men who have been through this planned, narcissistic isolation and destruction of their lives by their Asian brides. It is a narcissistic culture of using and disposing of people to further their own interests. It is a culturally accepted narcissistic business plan for these women. It is an unofficial part of the Thailand GDP. If the women do not feel inclined to do this, their husbands will beat them and pimp them until they do. They are expected to find an older Western partner who they know will die before them. Then they systematically isolate them from any surviving family or close friends, so there is no one with a claim on the assets. Then their money will have no one to contest it from their previous family or friends and will revert to their wive's real Thailand husbands and Thai families. The real Thai husband promotes this plan and manipulates their wives into it so that they can have an affluent lifestyle at the expense of the disposable Westerner husband. They see Westerners as total fools for falling for this narcissistic plan. It is a surprisingly successful long-term business plan for them and is seen as the only way that these families can escape abject poverty. The whole family, and indeed, everyone in the village, feels they are providing 'end of life' services to the Western husbands in exchange for financial benefits.

They seldom murder Western husbands as the death penalty looms large over the heads of any who dare. Instead, they are happy to achieve this by manipulating vulnerable men like me with the promise of true love and then waiting them out until they die of natural causes. Though it's not moral, taking advantage of stupidity is not illegal. The closest thing they do know to true love is the societal loyalty to their first husband and extended family members who they feel are relying upon them to support them. I am aware that some people will claim that I am a racist. I am not. I have always loved and studied Asian cultures and I am currently living within an Asian culture. But the fact is, there is a subculture that is narcissistic and is routinely praying on the vulnerable. It has become an ingrained and culturally acceptable form of narcissism. However, no form of narcissism is acceptable. Unless we talk about it, it will continue. It has to be spoken about. Openly, without fear of being accused of racism. I have to tell my story to other men in the hope that they will listen

The men who feel they are too smart to be manipulated, are the ones these Asian brides most easily ensnared. These Thai brides end up sacrificing men like me into a life of isolation and lies for their financial benefit. Yes, I know this is not exclusively a thing that happens only with Thai brides. It happens with most of the modern arranged marriages whether it is from Asian countries or Slavic countries. The plan is the same. The plan is narcissistic, selfish manipulation, and using one person for their benefit until that person dies.

True, I am living in a beautiful part of the world. So, I will make the best of the bad decisions I have made. I live and eat well. I'm been taking care of physically and I'm not afraid of being murdered, but part of me has died inside. Every time I see her disappear to the next village. I know that she is going to see her true husband. I realise that for a very smart man, I've made some dumb decisions.

It is my sincerest hope that I will be able to undo some of the damage that was done before I left Australia and reconnect with some of my Australian friends. Most especially with my dear daughter. Narcissistic abuse, never just affects just one vulnerable person. It affects the whole family. Dr. D'Montford is helping me to believe that recovery is possible. it is a one step at a time process. It is about repairing the damage you have allowed to happen to your own life, family and self. That self-esteem can be rebuilt, and then I may be able to thrive again.

Lillian's Story

You were my friend and marriage celebrant. You were on my side when nobody else was when I married into this crazy rich Asian family, even though I am Vietnamese, I have remained very much the outsider. I am the scapegoat in the family for anything that goes wrong. I am blamed for my husband's lack of success and unprofessional behaviour at work. I even get blamed for financial decisions I do not make within the family.

I often think about you but have refrained from contacting you since I know you are busy. We still keep and cherish the Marriage Knots.

My mother-in-law has interfered in our marriage and tried to control it. She thinks she knows better than both her own son and myself – even interfering between me and my child – stressing me to the point where I've had a miscarriage. This Sunday, I will be lighting candles and scattering flowers and candies for my unborn children (2 miscarriages) with my surviving son. I feel a powerful presence, a lingering grief.

I am the only person who has stood up to my mother-in-law and father-in-law in their entire lives. They are not used to people standing up to them because of their financial power. Everyone else is afraid of them, worried they will cut their family's or business's economic lifeline.

I asked a Life Coach to help me let go and forgive my mother-in-law. The process made me physically ill. I vomited out so much saliva and unseen stuff in a bucket after my session with her.

Then, after almost ten years, I forgave my mother-in-law and went to seek more help.

I appreciated your advice when you told me to:

> *"Make sure these people that you are forgiving have earned forgiveness; otherwise, they will do it to you again. It's not about punishing them; it's about respecting yourself and ensuring they understand you will not tolerate this behaviour in the future. You must ensure that you have total autonomy over yourself and that they can never have power over you again. When their behaviour improves, then you forgive them. If*

their behaviour does not improve, what's the point of forgiving them? Just don't until they do. Draw your line in the sand, then let them go to their own karma. That also prevents you from dropping to their level."

Yes, the daughter-in-law's job is to stand up to the mother-in-law. I know that you are glad that I did. And I heard what you said about forgiving too soon. I know you are so happy I got rid of the resentment, and I now understand that I will keep her at arm's length unless she earns forgiveness. I see how different my relationship is from your relationship with your three daughters-in-law. You have a good working relationship with them. You respect them and expect them to stand up to you for their husbands (your sons) and their point of view.

Respect has to be earned, and if she's not treating me respectfully, well...

Trust also has to be earned; the three go together: Respect, forgiveness, and then trust.

You are right...

- 1st Respect

- 2nd Forgiveness
- 3rd Trust

Since the beginning of this year, I have again kept her at arm's length. When the woman said, "I've tolerated enough of you. If I want to, I can separate both of you," I realised I trusted her too much. I thought she loved me as a daughter. It turns out it was only for the best interests of "her family assets." For her, money is more important than love.

I don't trust him anymore, as he has no respect for me. He formed an emotional bond with another woman. He didn't hide it. He flaunted it in front of me. No matter what we never leave our husbands or break up a family in my culture. Especially when there is a child. It is tough to trust a man any more after he has been so blatant about having an affair with a work colleague. You are spot on; I want justice; I felt injustice. That such a dishonourable woman could get protected by having had leukaemia years ago. She's recovered and is in complete remission; however, if it weren't for her leukaemia, then all around her would have treated her very differently. She plays the victim card so well to justify her bad behaviour. Narcissism by playing the victim. She gets away with doing whatever she wants. I believe she could get away with murder. It cons people. It sucks them right in. My mum and the mother-in-law said: "Leave her be; she doesn't have long to live." But this is rubbish. Absolute bullshit!

This woman was introduced to me in 2018 after she gave birth to her daughter, and it was recommended that we exchange numbers and befriend each other. I trusted her because she was married and had a 6-month-old daughter. December 20, 2020. I had a weekend lunch with her and my husband. Unsuspecting of anything. At that time, I thought she was a genuine sweet person and a good friend of my husband. A married woman with her daughter, the husband was "busy" and couldn't make it on the day. At the time, her poor husband was aware of her emotional infidelity and went to church a lot to pray or seek counselling. On Easter Sunday, 2021, we walked with her and her husband. I was suspicious because she and my husband's proximity was too close. She was nervous and kept giggling. In 2021, I found out she and my husband had an emotional affair, and my husband asked her to leave her husband for him. She cried and said no because she was married, but she continued to flirt with my husband even after I found out and confronted her six times.

She kept playing the professional victim, selling her Leukaemia story, that her husband and her family do not love her and neglect her. She was living in total Victim Consciousness to manipulate other people and get what she wanted—seeking favouritism and nepotism at work... including my husband. So narcissistic! This included her blatantly flirting with my husband on the phone and in front of my face to torment me after I confronted her. Eventually, she was told to desist from this unprofessional conduct in the workplace, and she flipped the situation. Taking advantage of the "Me Too Movement," she blamed my husband for sexual harassment. She was again casting herself as a victim.

The situation has come to a head in the workplace. About one month ago, I suspected that his mistress caused a schism between my husband and another person. That schism was high-risk and could have led either higher management to sack my husband, a CFO, or that other person, also a CFO.

The company HR has decided to strategically break down the team she is in, for which she is the Finance Manager. I think their main priority is to minimise risks and increase her workload to discourage her and make her volunteer to resign. Yesterday, her mother confronted me, accusing me of having caused the situation at work. It is interesting how the mother is also trying to blame me for her daughter's actions and won't let her daughter accept responsibility for her actions. She's so cunning, silent and malicious, playing the victim and pretending to be weak. She manipulated her own mother into a narcissistic attack on me. Her mother said: "You're lucky my daughter is weak; if it were any other strong woman, you would have lost your husband a long time ago."

You can imagine what effect this had on me. It sent me into a spin. I had to fight myself. It took me half a day to get out of my head. Yesterday, I worked very hard to maintain composure and restraint. I had to fight my urges to retaliate and let Karma unfold. The psychologist from 2020 to 2022 advised me to look at his mistress's photos occasionally and train my mind to the point that I am no longer affected by her and no longer have ill will or an aversion towards her.

I believe my husband has only acquired his narcissist characteristics from the stronger narcissists around him, i.e. his mother and his mistress.

I am still seeking therapy to overcome the traumas of the emotional affairs between them, shock, betrayal by this woman, cheated. What distresses me the most is that my husband did not consider how his abuse of me might affect his child. In our culture, if a husband and wife have a problem, discussing it in front of the children is not polite. However, my husband has often disrespected me in front of my young son. His witnessing his father's narcissistic abuse of me has had a disturbing effect on him. Please see the email from my son's child psychologist to our GP.

> *"Dear Dr Xxxxxx,*
> *RE: Axxxx Lxxxx*
> *Thank you for referring Master Axxxx Lxxxx to AXX for an ADHD assessment. Axxxx's mother has*

provided me with informed consent to communicate with you. He attended 4 sessions with me between 6 October 2023 and 27 October 2023. I have completed a clinical interview with Axxxx's mother and have completed a child screener. Based on the available information at this stage of our engagement, Axxxx did not present with any attentional disorders. Instead, he presented with symptoms consistent with F43.10 Post-traumatic Stress Disorder according to the DSM-5-TR in the context of ongoing familial conflict, witnessing domestic violence from his father, and causing his mother's miscarriage following punching her. He is already being bullied at school, which causes ongoing distress. He has displayed some re-enacting of violence by punching people and displaying emotional disregulation at home and at school. His mother is also under significant stress from her husband and various familial pressures. Cognitive Behavioural techniques are planned, involving psychoeducation and relaxation techniques.

I will continue working with Axxxx and will write back after our 6th session.

Sincerely Xxxxx"

My husband's behaviour significantly changed eight months after our son was born. He verbally abused me so much since 2019. By 2021, I was an emotional wreck. He found me crying in the pantry. Instead of compassion, he started in on me again. He laughed at my tears. "Well, you're the one that told me to go and find another wife." I couldn't take it any more, so I snapped and agreed to leave and told him I would go and see a divorce lawyer in the morning. His face darkened with hate. He looked like a different person. It was such a complete transformation it didn't even look human... like a petty, twisted, impish creature. "See! See! My mother was right about you! You are just in this relationship for the money. She knew that you would go back on your word. Didn't you say you will take nothing if you leave me?" Now I realise I have been guilt-tripped. I am slowly and safely cutting my etheric bond with him.

But at the time, I didn't have a voice. I literally lost my voice. I was screaming and crying in public and at home, but I didn't have a voice. I was advised to keep quiet and keep the secret if I wanted to save my family. Now and then, my husband and my mother-in-law will remind me to keep my promises. Do not leave, and if I do to take nothing. I know it is only a trick to manipulate me into keeping my words of honour, even if they don't keep their promises. When this happens, it makes me feel so sick in the stomach.

They even used my good deeds against me. For example, when I saved a family friend's marriage, that perhaps didn't deserve to be saved. He had an affair with another woman and bought a house for that woman. I was very disappointed in my friend and kept a safe distance from him while at the same time encouraging him to reconcile with his wife. His wife fully trusted me, and now we are good friends. Initially, he lied to me about how this had all come about. He tried to lie to me about his wife and character assassinated her so that he would look good if he decided to get rid of his wife. Eventually, I got him to be honest with me, then himself and finally his wife. My mother-in-law accused me of having more than friendship with this man than my own husband. Yet my husband admired what I tried to do until his mother got in his ear. My husband then told me that I didn't prioritise him or our family. When he had his affair, he used this, as well as many other positive things I had done, as excuses. It's like his mother was training him to be a narcissist and showing him how to abuse me narcissistically.

I feel like his mother has worked on his soul to produce a mini replica of her own twisted, tormenting evil. I see there is no point in trying to threaten her in return for her threats. That will only make her scheme more. It will only make her try to be more manipulative. Her mind and heart work differently from mine. I'm just reacting, trying to defend myself. She can think of many worse scenarios than I could ever throw at her in defence. I don't mean what I say when provoked, but she does. I see that it is much more powerful not to be drawn into her energy-draining games. She will keep pushing me until I react, and then she has something she can point to, to use against me, to try and tell my husband and others that I am bad. I am a good person, a very good person. But even good people will snap if constantly berated. Rather than defending myself when she is attributing evil motives to me, I can now see if I am just silent and stand back, keep my energy, and then I keep my energy and feel much better. She has nowhere to go with her threats and manipulations. That grey rock technique really works!

Women like that don't have any peace in their hearts. The more silent and strong I am, the more it feels like pouring hot coals on her forehead. However, I lose my power if I drop to her level and start threatening.

I am so tired but still have trouble sleeping. Cognitive Diffusion doesn't really work. Humanist Psychology is wishy-washy. The Gestalt therapy that you recommended, being a process-based therapy, really helps me to expend some of that emotional energy. It has made me feel calmer and released much of the burden I'm carrying so I can think and act more clearly.

I have been awake intermittently since 2am, but I lie in bed with my son and husband weighing on my mind. My recurring thoughts often vex me in the early morning, 3am to 5am, and I am often annoyed by the idea of them being disrespectful and deliberately tormenting me. Instead of desperately swallowing sleeping tablets to calm myself down, I would read about my various forms of anger and how to pray. If it's really bad, I will take natural sleeping tablets. If I can't sleep now, as you recommended, I get up and work on something or write. Like this, my story for your book. Here is some of the journaling that I've been doing:

> *To my husband,*
> *You might be abusive, but I choose not to be.*
> *You are unfaithful; I choose to be faithful.*
> *You might not love me; I choose to love you and our whole family—the bigger picture.*
> *You and your family can take extreme precautions out of fear; I choose to live with love and not be fearful. I prefer to live a dignified life.*

> To my husband, his mistress, and my Mother-in-Law,
>
> I will not stoop down to your level; I choose to live my life free from anxiety and fear.

I have promised myself that if they have not changed their behaviours, and I'm not keeping their word and are still victimising me after the 21st of November, 2023, I will consider engaging legal services.

Thank you for your advice. If only I had contacted you in 2021 instead.

2025 Update:

I chose to stay with my narcissistic husband within his narcissistic family. However, things have shifted because the way that I've reacted to them has shifted.

When my husband begins his narcissistic abuse or rants, I stop speaking to him. I remove myself from the situation. I pickup my handbag and leave the room or leave the house for approximately one hour. I go to a coffee shop or sometimes I will go to see a happy movie. (Once I even went to Vietnam for a month to do charity work.)

I come home happy. He is realising that his games are no longer working. That he doesn't get to steal my energy anymore. That his games don't make him feel better, they are making him feel worse. Instead they are making him feel insecure and vulnerable. He is making himself feel that way. It's been a bit like training a dog with negative reinforcement. When he barks and slathers, he only ends up choking himself at the end of his own chain rather than getting to enjoy taking a bite out of me, because I'm not there. For him, I believe he feels that 'the end of his chain' is getting shorter and shorter each time he tries unsuccessfully.

When I come back he is different. He is calmer. Even though he does not yet apologise. He often will have done some home maintenance or masculine thing around the house, which he is eager to show me and seek my praise for. This is a really big change.

The emotional affair with the woman at work has ceased. She was transferred to a different department and he was disgraced. For a short while my mother-in-law held me responsible for his disgrace. I refused to accept that responsibility and he had to wear the disgrace on his own shoulders. Though he still flirts with married women, I believe that his habits have changed in this regard.

My son seems happier at school and is less troubled.

I have let my husband know that I will not live in a situation where I am constantly abused. If he wants the family to stay together then he must take responsibility for his actions. He does not like hearing this. But I will not argue with him about it. I have told him. I think, because my recent reactions, he can see that I am serious. I hold my own energy and I hold my own space and I do not let him get to me.

My mother-in-law moved back to Singapore, as she felt frustrated that it became impossible to interfere in our marriage. Without me reacting to her she was no longer successful.

One other interesting thing has begun to occur. When my husband does try to victimise me either verbally or physically, karma seems to be happening more quickly for him. He injures himself or gets sick afterwards. After being injured or sick, he seems to treat me with greater respect, as if the ancestors really are looking after me. I personally feel that when his energy gets low, if he doesn't get an energy hit from picking a fight from me, that his low energy is allowing these things to happen to himself. Either way he is beginning to realise that our life together is better for him if he treats me better.

This is not the deep love and consideration that I crave and deserve. However, it is something that I can tolerate if I choose to stay in this relationship and honour my traditional obligations within this family.

Again thank you for my all the support. It has allowed me to go stronger. Thank you for being the only therapist who did not abandon me when I expressed strongly that I chose to honour my traditional values and stay in this relationship. Thank you for helping me grow stronger and develop my coping mechanisms, that have allowed me to become more empowered and thus my relationship has become more liveable. I thank you for helping me grow stronger, move out of the victim role and helping my family stay together.

Blessings to you

Lillian

Can a Narcissist Change and Recover?

We acknowledge that many people may want to stay in a narcissistic relationship and try to help their partner recover. We acknowledge this, but cannot recommend it. Narcissistic victims must be very cautious about being the helper/rescuer. Narcissistic victims often follow this pattern of trying to fix or rescue their partner. If you go down this path you must expect your partner to put in equal or greater effort than you to rectify the issues in this relationship. **You cannot fix this relationship just by your efforts alone.**

If someone you interact with regularly shows narcissistic patterns, it's not up to you to change them. Better for you to focus on how you can change the dance you do with that person. Anyone, if angry enough, can display narcissistic traits. Yet, you must choose to not let yourself be intimidated or controlled by fear of anger. Just gracefully leave the situation for a cool-down period, get a drink of water, and then return for a calm conversation. The occasional angry disagreement is very different from the continuous emotional roller-coaster ride of a manipulative narcissist.

No person should allow themselves to continue living in a situation with someone who is continually angry and where they are a continuous victim. It is not the victim's job to 'fix" their partner. However, the narcissist will try to convince their partner that it is. It is like dealing with a drug addict. They have to want to recover, and you have to be very careful to not become their enabler.

The victim needs to acknowledge that no change will happen unless the narcissist themselves acknowledges that they have a serious problem, that they are in the wrong and are willing to seek professional help. Even under these circumstances, it may be best and safest to move to live at a safe distance, until you can see that real progress over time has been accomplished.

The Consequences of Staying With a Narcissist

Good consequences show that you have made a good decision. Conversely, negative consequences are the result of poor decision-making, When it comes to being in a relationship with a narcissist, the consequences can be devastating.

Self-Worth

When you're in a relationship with a narcissist, your self-worth takes a hit. Narcissists are masters at putting the blame on others and making them feel like they are never good enough. Over time, you start to believe them. You might even start to think that you deserve the way they treat you.

Emotional Abuse

Narcissists are also experts at emotional abuse. They will say things to try to control you or make you feel bad about yourself. They might even threaten to hurt themselves or others if you don't do what they want. Narcissists can be very convincing, and it's easy to believe them when they say these things.

Being in a relationship with a narcissist can also lead to something called the "cycle of abuse." This is when the narcissist hurts you, then feels bad about it, and tries to make up for it by being very nice to you. This cycle can repeat itself over and over again, and it can be very difficult to break free from it.

Guilt

Another consequence of being in a relationship with a narcissist is guilt. Narcissists are often very good at making you feel guilty, even when it's not your fault. They might say things like, "If you loved me, you would do this for me," or "I can't believe you would do this to me."

These kinds of statements can make you feel guilty and like you're always doing something wrong.

Isolation

Narcissists also tend to isolate their partners from their friends and family. This is because they want to control them and have them all to themselves. They might say things like, "Your friends don't care about you," or "You don't need your family, I'm all you need."

Can Anything Be Done?

When it comes to being in a relationship with a narcissist, it can be difficult to see any hope for change. Narcissists are some of the most stuck-in-their-ways individuals out there. They tend to believe that they are always right and that everyone else is wrong. This lack of flexibility can make it seem impossible to have a healthy, productive relationship with them.

However, there are some things you can do to try and improve the situation. If you are committed to making things work, then it is worth trying out some of these tips:

Open Communication

One of the most important things you can do in any relationship is to communicate openly and honestly with each other. This is especially important when you are dealing with a narcissist. Narcissists tend to shut down or become defensive when they feel like they are being attacked.

If you can open up the lines of communication, it will be easier to discuss difficult topics without triggering a fight. You may need to be the one to initiate these conversations, but it will be worth it in the long run.

Boundaries

Another important thing to remember when you are in a relationship with a narcissist is to set boundaries. It is important that you nurture your own needs and wants and do not allow yourself to be steamrolled by your partner.

Narcissists can be very manipulative and controlling. If you do not set clear boundaries, they will take advantage of you. By setting boundaries, you are telling your partner that you are not going to put up with their bad behaviour.

Keep Your Expectations Realistic

It is also important to keep your expectations realistic when you are in a relationship with a narcissist. You need to be realistic about what you can and cannot change about your partner. If you expect too much from them, you are bound to be disappointed.

Focus on the Positive

Finally, try to focus on the positive aspects of your relationship. It can be easy to get caught up in all the negative things about being in a relationship with a narcissist.

However, there are also some good things about it. Narcissists can be very charming and charismatic. They can also be exciting and fun to be around. If you can focus on the positive aspects of your relationship, it will help you to cope with the negative ones.

Helping Them to Change

If you want to help your narcissistic partner to change, then you need to be patient and understanding. It is not going to happen overnight and it may never happen at all. You also need to be prepared for the possibility that your efforts may not be successful. If you are not prepared for this, then you are setting yourself up for disappointment.

However, if you are willing to put in the work, then there is a chance that you can help your partner to change. They may never be completely cured of their narcissism, but they may be able to develop more healthy coping mechanisms. This can make a big difference in the quality of your relationship.

Quick Fixes

Here are three quick fixes to try. These are about engaging a positive response from your partner. If your partner wants to overcome their issues and puts in an effort to try some of these with you then there is hope. Ultimately you need to move them towards professional help with a therapist who is skilled and experienced in dealing with narcissistic personality disorder. Remember, if they do not want to work with you on these issues, you have to determine how long you will tolerate unapologetic bad behaviour. It is painful and damaging to continue to live long-term with somebody with this disorder. Your narcissistic partner may express that they feel helpless when you are upset. May not know what to do because they may not have had an opportunity to learn soothing responsiveness to human pain. Fortunately, positive responses for helping distressed others can be learned. However, keep in mind that it takes two people to make a relationship work and one to wreck it. You must expect to see effort from your partner, if not, this is not going to work.

Training Your Partner to Calm Down

Dr Susan Heitler PhD makes two suggestions based upon conflict resolution techniques :

1. Implement early exits from conversations at the first signs of emerging anger.

"If you cease to engage in arguments, there will no longer be arguments. By contrast, if you stay and keep talking with someone who shows signs of anger, you are taking an enabling role toward their anger. To exit, stand, start walking, pleasantly excuse yourself to go get a drink of water, and exit the room. Return as soon as you feel calm. Initiate positive conversation on a safe topic before returning eventually to the difficult issue."

"How do I deal with my partner's sudden anger and outbursts?" It is an important topic to deal with as I have been asked about this issue more than any other issue when partners are trying to deal with a narcissistic partner. The most important thing is that you must communicate to them that these angry behaviours are not acceptable and that if they continue, long-term you will not remain in the relationship.

Don't be reactive. Have your action plan ready so that you cannot be pulled into a reactive situation. Learn to recognise early indicators and remove yourself from a situation before it escalates.

You must step out and calm down and not be drawn into being angry yourself. Many narcissistic abuses will use your induced anger as an excuse for their bad behaviour. It can be a game for them to try and get the non-angry person angry and out of control. Anger creates relationships based on coercion, not love or cooperation.

Angry outbursts can quickly become bullying. If they are making you feel like a victim it is very hard to not lash out at your apparent attacker. Don't try to get back at them. This escalates the cycle. Anger drives the continual chaos and drama of a partner's narcissistic personality disorder.

Allowing them to get you angry can make you feel depressed. Replace angry reactions with the development of exit and self-soothing strategies. go out and get a cuppa. Go to a supportive friend's house go to the movies.

Learn to stay in the calm zone. Interact with a narcissistic partner *only* when both of you are cool calm and collected. Return to the triggering dialogue only if absolutely necessary, when you feel calm enough to stay calm and collaborative.

2. When your partner does not listen to what you said, first digest aloud and validate his or her alternative perspective. Then, put yours back on the table. Become an expert in "Yes, and at the same time..."

A: "I'd love to go out to see a funny movie tonight."
B: "There's no way I want to go out. I'm too tired."
*A: "**Yes**, I can see you're tired. **And at the same time**, I'm up for enjoying something funny. I'd be glad to pick a movie we could watch together at home. Then, if you're too tired, you could just go to sleep. How*

would you feel about watching an old Charlie Chaplin flick with me?"

This agree-and-add strategy enables you to give your partner a second and even third opportunity to hear you.

In addition, after your not-so-good-at-listening partner feels heard, they are more likely to be able to relax enough to be able to hear your perspective as well.

Training Your Partner to Listen

A key approach to narcissism is to train your partner to listen by letting them come to realise that you will not tolerate not being listened to. Narcissists block information about others' feelings.

Ask your partner to stop using the word BUT when you are disagreeing. 'But' negates your reaching an understanding. It subtracts, dismisses, and eliminates whatever came before. Get them to use Dr Susan Heitler's PhD preferred phrase: *and at the same time*. This moves things from a single self-centred perspective to a dualistic perspective, allowing them to see that there is more than one point of view here. It is very hard for people with narcissistic personality disorder to see the viewpoint of other people. That way, instead of indulging in the narcissistic pattern of ignoring and disputing another's viewpoint, they may begin to see additional viewpoints. However, it is only through long-term persistence insistence, and great effort from both of you, that they may begin to see that in this relationship there are two points of view here that matter.

When a partner expresses a differing point of view they feel as if you are making them "wrong." If you feel angry anxious or sad, the narcissistic response is to personalise. They take the feelings of others as critical statements about themselves. For a narcissist, it is, "all about me," so what you are feeling and expressing must be about them as well. Therefore, narcissists get angry instead of supportive when their partner disagrees with them or experiences negative emotions. If they jump to conclusions, especially angry conclusions, you need to pull them up in their tracks. You need to remain as emotionally neutral as possible, whilst you clearly tell them that they have not heard, or understood, what you have said and therefore you need them to understand this is not about them, it's about is about your point of view which differs from theirs.

Additionally, when things are calm you need to tell them that for you to stay in a relationship you need to have your point of view heard and respected. You may help them accomplish this by asking them questions like:

- Can you see how my concerns are different from your own?
- What do you understand about what I am thinking and feeling?
- Do you understand my feelings on this issue? If so can you please give a response that indicates that you do or repeat back to me what you think I have said? This can be quite an eye-opener for a partner as a narcissist's internal dialogue is often very different to the conversation you were trying to have with them.
- Is there anything in my perspective that you can agree with?
- What makes sense to you about my perspective?

If they go back to talking about their perspective, bring them back to yours. Point out that the two perspectives are different and that you need them to take your perspective seriously. You may need to do this two or three times. However, if they are not getting the point of the conversation or refuse to listen, or if it begins to escalate towards frustration and anger, you will have to walk away from the conversation and try it again another time.

3. Radiate sunshine.

> Susan Heitler's final suggestion is this: *"We all function well when we feel loved and valued. The more agreement, appreciation, smiles, affection, hugs, and other positives you shower on each other, the happier you both will be."*

This is great and I hope it does work. I know that this is what a lot of people in narcissistic relationships are hoping for. That their good behaviour will somehow transform their partner to behave in a better way. It can happen if their partner is actively wanting to change. **All relationships are compromise.** However, if your attempts at staying positive and affectionate are met with anger, aggression and dismal behaviour, then withdraw your energy from this relationship. Do not reinforce negative behaviour by tolerating it. You do not have to continuously tolerate abuse. Compromise is good, but you must not compromise yourself. Compromise is different to putting up with abuse. Compromise is where two people come up with a workable solution. Two people can want two different things, but negotiating a compromise is where you come up with a third option. Something that is not entirely the idea of one person or the other but where it meets somewhere in the middle. It may feel like a two-step forward, one-step back situation. As long as there is forward motion there is hope.

You do not want to be going over and over the same ground again and again. It is not about you just forgiving something they have done, only to have them turn around and do it again straight away. This is not a compromise and this is not them putting in any effort. Draw your line in the sand and if your partner goes too far you must step back. People with narcissistic personality disorder often go too far. There are some things in a relationship that cannot be overcome or undone. There are some things in arguments that can never be answered. Some things when they have been said cannot be unsaid. If damage is being created, you must step back. Additionally, you should not allow your partner to bring your mood down. If you are a naturally happy, sunny, person and you're in a naturally happy sunny mood and they want to be abysmal then leave and go somewhere with some other people where you can be happy and sunny and enjoy yourself. Do not stay around a person who is going to bring you down in an attempt to keep you under control.

The bottom line is, that you can only help a narcissist recover if they are willing to commit to their recovery. Yes, that ultimately means committing to regular professional therapy. It will take two people in a relationship to make it work. One can destroy it. If they are bent on destruction, you do not have to stay on that path with them.

Last Resort

If you have tried all of these things and nothing has worked, then you have to understand that you need to leave the relationship. This is not something to be taken lightly, but sometimes it is the only option.

If you are in an abusive or toxic relationship with a narcissist, then it is important to get out for your safety. No one deserves to be treated badly, no matter how much you love them.

Therefore, try to identify any narcissistic traits in a new potential partner, before getting too emotionally attached to someone, it is important to be aware of the potential risks involved in being in a relationship with a narcissist.

Keep Your Love to Yourself for a While

Leaving and asking for help does not mean to go and frantically in search of another love. Right now, you're still sorting this out. So don't rush out looking for a new love. Love will not rescue you. Only you can do that for yourself. Love will happen. Love always happens. It will happen again for you… but not right now. Wait!

The solution for you is not to fall immediately into another relationship. If you do that without full recovery, as we have shown you, by our personal experiences, you WILL just end up repeating the pattern. Stop believing that love will bring you joy. I know this flies in the face of every rom/com you have ever watched. But that is the fiction and this is the truth; Find your joy and then you will find a good relationship.

Love is not a drug that you need to score to make you feel happy. That is an emotional addiction. You don't need that endorphin rush right now. Have the occasional chocolate instead. But, don't fall back into your old addictive love patterns. You need time to form newer healthier patterns. Find your joy and then you will find a good relationship.

Just for now, call "Time Out" on relationships.

This will be hard but you can do it… (just until you get your joy back anyway!)

Do Not Lose Hope

There are so many beautiful loving people in this world seeking a loving and supportive partner. The vast majority of people in this world are good people. Start to cultivate friendships with good people as it is amongst the company of good people that you will find a good person to share your life. Recover, move on, find your joy. You do not have to endure victimisation to find the path to love. Victims attract victimisers. So don't play the victim. People find martyrs annoying. Historically, martyrs get nailed to crosses. Get help, heal and move forward. Move towards those who are willing to put in effort to earn your love and respect. Respect yourself enough to only allow yourself to be loved and nurtured and you will find yourself in a loving relationship with someone who respects you.

After Word

Don't ever think that there is nobody out there for you.

Don't ever think that you are alone.

I love you. Writing this book for you was an act of love. It was an act of love for you and it was an act of self-love for me – Because, hey, I've been there. Right where you are now. I want you to know I've come out the other side and you can too. You will if you just implement these simple steps.

You can come out the other side better than what you were before.

You cannot be alone. This whole immense universe exists to support you. You could not be here if the planets weren't spinning in their orbits around an immense Sun. The seasons move through their cycles around this beautiful planet, every plant, every flower, every oxygen molecule, the very ground that you stand on supports your life now.

You are important to the universe. You can never be separated from it, no matter what you do. And you are important to me. I am here for you and I want you to thrive. Do it for me. But above all do it for yourself. You are worthy and you deserve your best life now.

Every blessing to you as you move forward into your amazing new future.

With much love for you always.

Shé

www.ingramcontent.com/pod-product-compliance
Lightning Source LLC
Chambersburg PA
CBHW071149070526
44584CB00019B/2721